The Impact and Cost of Taxation in Canada
The Case for Flat Tax Reform

The Impact and Cost of Taxation in Canada

The Case for Flat Tax Reform

edited by Jason Clemens

The Fraser Institute

www.fraserinstitute.org

2008

Editing, design, and production: Lindsey Thomas Martin
Cover design by Bill Ray
Image for front cover: ©Adam Korzekwa, iStockphoto

Date of issue: February 2008
Printed and bound in Canada

Library and Archives Canada Cataloguing in Publication Data

The impact and cost of taxation in Canada: the case for flat tax reform / edited by Jason Clemens.

Includes bibliographical references.
ISBN 978–0–88975–229–0

1. Taxation--Canada.   2. Flat-rate income tax--Canada.   I. Clemens, Jason.

HJ2449.I56 2008   336.2'050971   C2008-900683-6

Contents

About the authors

Patrick Basham

Patrick Basham teaches in the Government Department at the Johns Hopkins University. He is Founding Director of the Democracy Institute, a research organization based in Washington, DC. Mr Basham previously served as a Senior Fellow at the Cato Institute, where he is currently an Adjunct Scholar. Prior to joining Cato, he served as the Director of the Social Affairs Centre at The Fraser Institute. He has written and edited books, scholarly articles, and studies on a variety of domestic and foreign-policy topics, including campaign finance, democratization, education reform, obesity, political marketing, and the regulation of risk. A frequent media commentator, his articles have appeared in the *New York Times, Washington Post, Forbes, Sunday Telegraph, The Independent, Australian Financial Review, National Post,* and *Globe & Mail.* Mr Basham earned his B.A., M.A., and Ph.D. degrees in Political Science from Carleton University, the University of Houston, and Cambridge University, respectively.

Jason Clemens

Jason Clemens is the Director of Research Quality and a Resident Scholar in Fiscal Studies at The Fraser Institute. He also acts as the Director of Strategic Planning and Budgeting within the Institute. He has an Honours Bachelors Degree of Commerce and a Masters' Degree in Business Administration from the University of Windsor as well as a post-Baccalaureate Degree in Economics from Simon Fraser University. He has published over 40 major studies on a wide range of topics, including taxation, government spending, labour market regulation, banking, welfare reform, productivity, entrepreneurship, Public Choice economics, and economic prosperity. He has published over 200 shorter articles, which have appeared in such newspapers as the *Wall Street Journal, Investors Business Daily, National Post, Globe & Mail, Toronto Star, Vancouver Sun, Calgary Herald, Ottawa Citizen, Montreal Gazette*, and *La Presse*. Mr. Clemens has been a guest on numerous radio programs across the country and has appeared on the *CBC National News, CTV News, CBC Business Newsworld*, CBC's *CounterSpin*, Global TV, BCTV, and Report on Business TV as an economic commentator. He has appeared before committees of both the House of Commons and the Senate as an expert witness. In 2006, he received the prestigious *Canada's Top 40 Under 40* award presented by Caldwell Partners as well as an Odyssey award from the University of Windsor.

Kumi Harischandra

Kumi Harischandra is a Research Economist in the Fiscal Studies Department at The Fraser Institute. She holds a Bachelor of Social Sciences (Honours) degree in Economics from the National University of Singapore and a Master of Arts degree in Economics from Simon Fraser University. Since joining the Institute as a Research Intern in 2006 and subsequently as a full-time researcher in 2007, Ms. Harischandra has written on several policy issues such as taxation, government spending, foreign investment, poverty, charitable giving and business attitudes. Her recent co-publications include *Beyond Equalization: Examining Fiscal Transfers in a Broader Context* (2007) and contributions to *Fraser Forum*.

Daniel Mitchell

Daniel J. Mitchell is a Senior Fellow at the Cato Institute in Washington, DC. A top expert on tax reform and fiscal policy, Mr. Mitchell is a strong advocate of a flat tax and international tax competition. Prior to joining Cato, he was a senior fellow with The Heritage Foundation and an economist for Senator Bob Packwood and the Senate Finance Committee. He also served on the 1988 Bush/Quayle transition team and was Director of Tax and Budget Policy for Citizens for a Sound Economy. His articles can be found in such publications as the *Wall Street Journal, New York Times, Investor's Business Daily*, and

Washington Times. He is a frequent guest on radio and television and a popular speaker on the lecture circuit. Mitchell holds bachelor's and master's degrees in economics from the University of Georgia and a Ph.D. in economics from George Mason University.

Milagros Palacios

Milagros Palacios is a Senior Research Economist in the Fiscal Studies Department at The Fraser Institute. She holds a Bachelors degree in Industrial Engineering from the Pontifical Catholic University of Peru and an M.Sc. in Economics from the University of Concepción, Chile. She is co-author of the *Measuring Labour Markets in Canada and the United States* (2007), *Fiscal Performance Index* (2007), *Tax Freedom Day* (2007), *Canadian Provincial Investment Climate Report* (2007), *An Empirical Comparison of Labour Relations Laws in Canada and the United States* (2006), *Union Disclosure in Canada and the United States* (2006), *Canadian Government Debt* (2006), and *Transparency of Labour Relations Boards in Canada and the United States* (2005). Her recent commentaries have appeared in such newspapers as the *National Post* and *Windsor Star*. Since joining the Institute, Ms. Palacios has written regularly for *Fraser Forum* on a wide range of topics including labour regulation, fiscal issues, taxation, charitable giving, and a host of environmental issues such as air quality, Kyoto, and water transfers.

Alvin Rabushka

Dr. Alvin Rabushka, the David and Joan Traitel Senior Fellow at the Hoover Institution, works in the public policy areas of taxation in the United States and abroad, economic development in the Pacific Rim countries, and the economies of Central and Eastern Europe. He is the author or coauthor of more than 20 books in the areas of race and ethnicity, aging, taxation, state and local government finances, and the economic development of Hong Kong and the "Asian tigers" of Taiwan, Korea and Singapore.

Dr. Rabushka has published numerous articles in scholarly journals and in such popular outlets as the *Wall Street Journal*, *New York Times*, and *Fortune*. He has consulted for, and testified before, a number of public agencies including the US Senate Committee on the Judiciary,

Joint Economic Committee of the Congress, House Ways and Means Committee, Senate Finance Committee, 1981 White House Conference on Aging, and the Agency for International Development. In 1980, he served on President Ronald Reagan's Tax Policy Task Force.

His books and articles on the flat tax (with Robert E. Hall) provided the intellectual foundation for numerous flat-tax bills that were introduced in Congress during the 1980s and 1990s and the proposals of several presidential candidates in 1996 and 2000. He was recognized in *Money* magazine's twentieth-anniversary issue "Money Hall of Fame" for the importance of his flat-tax proposal in bringing about passage of the *Tax Reform Act* of 1986. He has lectured on tax policy in Hong Kong, Israel, El Salvador, Guatemala, Mexico, Argentina, Chile, Canada, the Czech Republic, Austria, Italy, Sweden, Switzerland, and other countries. His pioneering work on the flat tax contributed to the adoption of the flat tax in 1994 in Estonia, followed by Latvia, Lithuania, Russia, Ukraine, Serbia, Romania, Slovakia, and Georgia. The flat tax is also under consideration in Croatia, Slovenia, and the Czech Republic.

Rabushka received his A.B. in Far Eastern studies from Washington University (St. Louis) in 1962, followed by his M.A. and Ph.D. degrees in political science from Washington University in 1966 and 1968. He spent 1963 in Hong Kong learning Chinese and 1966/1967 in Malaysia for research on his doctoral dissertation. He taught at the University of Rochester (1968–1976) and the University of Hong Kong (1973). He joined the Hoover Institution in 1976.

François Vaillancourt

François Vaillancourt has been a professor in the department of economic sciences at the University of Montreal since 1976. He completed his Ph.D. in economics at Queen's University in 1978. Professor Vaillancourt has been a guest lecturer at the University of Toronto and Australian National University and a research scholar at the Institute for Research in Public Policy (1992–2000) and the CD Howe Institute (2000–2003). Professor Vaillancourt was also the coordinator of research for the MacDonald Commission (1983–1986). He has consulted for a number of international organizations such as the

World Bank, OECD, UNDP, and national agencies such as Statistics Canada, Finance Canada, and the Séguin Commission. His fields of research include linguistic policies, intergovernmental financial relations, and tax compliance costs. He has published on a wide variety of issues including equalization in federal countries, education, minority language policies, federalism, and taxation. Professor Vaillancourt is widely acknowledged as one of the pre-eminent scholars on the issue of tax compliance and administrative costs.

Niels Veldhuis

Niels Veldhuis is Director of Fiscal Studies at The Fraser Institute. Since joining the Institute in 2002, he has authored or co-authored three books and 29 comprehensive studies on a wide range of topics including taxation, productivity, entrepreneurship, labor markets, and government failure. Mr. Veldhuis has written over 100 articles, which have appeared in over 40 newspapers including the *National Post, Globe & Mail,* and *Wall Street Journal.* He appears regularly on radio and television programs across the country and has appeared before committees of both the House of Commons and the Senate as an expert witness. Mr. Veldhuis received a Bachelor degree in Business Administration, with joint majors in business and economics, and a Master Degree in Economics from Simon Fraser University.

Acknowledgments

We would like to acknowledge and thank the Mitchell family and the John and Lotte Hecht Foundation for their financial support of this project. Without their support, this project could not have been undertaken and completed. The authors would also like to express their gratitude to a number of people and organizations that aided in different aspects of the volume over the last year and a half. A special thanks to Mr. Doug Bruce and the Canadian Federation of Independent Business (CFIB) for allowing access to their 2005 survey data on business tax compliance costs and for working collaboratively with the authors of the chapter on the data analysis. In addition, the authors would like to thank two anonymous business organizations that operate in the area of tax preparation. Their confidential data and assistance was vital to the completion of the section on tax compliance.

The authors would like to acknowledge the following people for their formal review of chapters of this book: Professor Jonathan Kesselman of Simon Fraser University, Professor Jack Mintz of the University of Toronto, Professor Chris Evans of Atax and the University of New South Wales (Australia), David Perry of the Canadian Tax Foundation, Niels Veldhuis, Director of Fiscal Studies and the Centre for Tax Studies at the Fraser Institute, Professor Ronald Kneebone of the University of Calgary, Professor David Andolfatto of Simon Fraser University, Dr. Daniel Mitchell, Senior Fellow in Fiscal Studies at the Cato Institute, and Professor Herbert Grubel, Professor Emeritus of Simon Fraser University. Their comments and suggestions were invaluable in completing this study. Any remaining errors, omissions, or mistakes are the sole responsibility of the authors. We would also like to express our thanks to Keith Godin and Kumi Harischandra for their assistance in various aspects of this volume. As the authors have worked indepen-dently, the views and analysis expressed in this document remain those of the authors and do not necessarily represent those of the supporters, trustees, or other staff at the Fraser Institute.

Foreword

Jason Clemens

There is increasing interest in, and recognition of, the need for both tax reduction and tax reform in Canada. Witness the major political parties in Canada, both federally and in various provincial capitals, arguing about how best to reduce taxes. The underlying assumption of these debates is that Canada not only needs tax cuts but must ensure that the right taxes are reduced in order to achieve a more efficient tax system that improves the Canadian economy. This book is dedicated to providing both the rationale for tax reform and a road map for that reform. The book includes five chapters from leading experts in the field and provides a persuasive, compelling case for tax reform in Canada.

1 ◆ *The Impact of Taxes on Economic Behavior*
The first chapter of this volume reviews the extensive academic and scholarly research on the economic effects of taxation. The Impact of Taxes on Economic Behavior by Fraser Institute economists, Milagros Palacios and Kumi Harischandra, offers a broad overview of the incentive effects associated with taxes that affect our decisions to work more, to save, to invest, and to engage in entrepreneurial activity. The chapter provides a powerful foundation from which to ask other pertinent questions regarding Canada's current tax system and its future.

2 ◆ *Tax Efficiency*

The second chapter of the book examines the efficiency of different taxes. Tax Efficiency by Jason Clemens, a resident scholar in fiscal studies at The Fraser Institute, and Niels Veldhuis, the director of fiscal studies at The Fraser Institute, compares the economic costs of different taxes based on differing incentive-based effects. The underlying premise of the analysis is that not all taxes are equal. That is, that some taxes impose much lower economic costs on society and should therefore be used to a greater extent while other taxes impose much larger costs and should be used less.

The chapter employs a standard methodology used for assessing the efficiency costs of different taxes: marginal efficiency cost (MEC). It calculates the cost of raising one additional dollar of tax revenue using different types of taxes. Estimates of the marginal efficiency costs of both American and Canadian taxes indicate that consumption and payroll (wage and salary) taxes are much less costly (and thus more efficient) than taxes on capital. For example, a study in 1997 by the Canadian Department of Finance for the Organisation for Economic Co-operation and Development concluded that corporate income taxes imposed a marginal cost of $1.55 (MEC) for each additional dollar of revenue compared to $0.17 for an additional dollar of revenue raised through consumption taxes. Other Canadian studies as well as estimates of the MEC of select US taxes are also presented in the chapter, which also indicate significant variation in the economic costs of different taxes and support the Canadian findings.

The chapter then presents data on the tax mix maintained by Canada and other industrialized countries (OECD countries) showing that Canada is an outlier in terms of its reliance on economically costly taxes and limited use of more efficient (less costly) taxes. Specifically, Canadian governments collected 46.5% of total tax revenues from income and profit taxes, the fourth highest reliance on these taxes (high marginal cost) among OECD countries. On the other hand, sales taxes, which are one of the most efficient type of taxes, accounts for only 25.9% of total tax revenues ranking Canada 24th out of 30 OECD countries in terms of its reliance on taxes on goods and services.

The clear implication is that Canada possesses an opportunity not only to reduce the tax burden but also to make our tax system far more efficient by shifting our use of taxes away from costly taxes (personal income and capital-based taxes) towards more efficient taxes (consumption).

3 ◆ *Compliance and Administrative Costs of Taxation in Canada*

The third chapter, Compliance and Administrative Costs of Taxation in Canada by François Vaillancourt, a renowned economics professor at the University of Montreal, and Jason Clemens provides readers with an understanding of the vast costs associated with administering, and complying with, our current tax system. The costs associated with any tax system are not simply the direct costs of paying taxes and the economic effects associated with taxes discussed previously. There are also the costs imposed on individuals and businesses to comply with tax regulations and the costs incurred by government in maintaining the tax-collection system.

The work presented in this chapter shows that tax compliance costs for individuals and businesses in Canada ranged from $16.2 billion to $25.0 billion in 2005 depending on the specific methodology employed. Administrative costs added another $2.7 billion to $5.8 billion. Thus, total compliance and administrative costs in Canada for 2005 ranged between $18.9 billion and $30.8 billion, representing between 1.4% and 2.3% of GDP. The results in the chapter show that individuals and businesses incur significant costs to comply with the tax system and governments spend significant resources administering the tax system.

4 ◆ *Lessons from Abroad—Flat Tax in Practice*

Chapter 4 is the first of two chapters specifically examining tax reform based on a flat-tax model. In this first chapter, Lessons from Abroad—Flat Tax in Practice, Dr. Patrick Basham of the Democracy Institute (formerly of the Cato Institute) and Dr. Daniel Mitchell of the Cato Institute explain how flat-tax systems are not just theoretical musings by professors in ivory towers but are, in fact, being used around the world.

The chapter describes how a host of diverse countries and jurisdictions ranging from Jersey (1940) to Hong Kong (1947) to Russia (2001) to the Czech Republic (2008) have adopted flat-tax systems with extraordinary success. The evidence presented by the authors is persuasive: the citizens in these reforming countries enjoy economic benefits that include stronger economic growth, higher overall tax receipts, and a generally more robust economy. This chapter provides readily observable evidence regarding the real-life benefits of a flat tax and the potential benefits available to citizens in countries or jurisdictions that reform their systems using such a model.

Interestingly, one of the aspects tackled by the authors is the move by former Soviet countries—including Estonia, Latvia, Lithuania, Russia, Serbia, Slovakia, Ukraine, Romania, Georgia—to adopt flat taxes. One of the insights gained from this section of the chapter is the resistance by special-interest groups to tax reform that forms a significant barrier to improvement. The reason these former Soviet-states were able to reform their tax systems, according to the authors, is that no such built-in special interests had developed. The governments in these countries were more able to design tax systems aimed at promoting broad economic progress while satisfying key aspects of tax policy such as fairness, simplicity, and efficiency rather than placating narrow special interests. This portion of the chapter provides a powerful explanation why so many countries, including Canada, experience strong and organized resistance to fundamental reform of the tax system.

5 ◈ A Flat Tax for Canada

The final chapter of the book, A Flat Tax for Canada, is by Alvin Rabushka, a renowned and pioneering Stanford University professor and the David and Joan Traitel Senior Fellow at the Hoover Institution, and by Niels Veldhuis. Professor Rabushka's books and articles on the flat tax (with Professor Robert E. Hall) have provided the intellectual foundation for a number of flat-tax reform bills in the United States during the 1980s and 1990s as well as for several proposals by presidential candidates in 1996 and 2000. His pioneering work on the flat tax has contributed to the adoption of the flat tax in Estonia, Latvia, Lithuania, Russia, Ukraine, Serbia, Romania, Slovakia, and Georgia.

This chapter may prove to be a watershed in tax reform in Canada as it provides a comprehensive and thorough case for adopting a flat tax in Canada. First, the chapter demolishes many, if not all, of the falsehoods about the flat tax and explains how it achieves the core goals of taxation: efficiency, fairness (equity), and simplicity.

More importantly, however, the chapter presents a detailed explanation of what a flat tax would look like for individual Canadians and Canadian businesses. The authors calculate that without reducing revenues to the federal government, a flat tax of 15.0% could be implemented covering both individuals and businesses. Obviously reducing federal spending and the accordant taxes required to pay for it would result in a lower rate. The chapter explains in detail how such a system would operate, considering some of the traditionally thorny issues such as depreciation, financial institutions, and international businesses.

Chapter five also presents a model for flat taxes for the Canadian provinces using the same flat-tax system suggested for the federal government. Provincial flat-tax rates range from a low of 6.1% in Newfoundland and Labrador to 15.5% in Québec. Western Canadian provinces would require among the lowest provincial flat-tax rates with Alberta at 6.8%, Saskatchewan at 7.5%, and British Columbia at 7.9%. Thus, overall combined federal-provincial flat tax rates would range from 21.1% in Newfoundland and Labrador to 28.5% in Québec.

Conclusion

The contributions by the authors involved in this project are critical to understanding why Canadians would benefit enormously from tax reform and, in particular, reform based on a flat tax. The authors hope that this book will stimulate an honest and open debate about the benefits of tax reform. The benefits available to Canadians and the economy as a whole from flat tax reform are substantial and lasting, including marked improvements in our tax system and the incentives people and businesses face regarding work effort, savings, investment, and entrepreneurship.

The Impact and Cost of Taxation in Canada
The Case for Flat Tax Reform

Chapter 1

The Impact of Taxes on Economic Behavior

Milagros Palacios & Kumi Harischandra

Though economists differ on many issues, there are a few basic concepts on which virtually all agree. One of the most important is the concept that people respond to incentives: people make decisions by comparing the costs and benefits of a particular action. When either the costs or benefits change, people's behavior also changes. For instance, when the price of a certain good rises, consumers will likely purchase it less and purchase alternatives (i.e. other goods) in its place. Similarly, when the price of an input rises, businesses will search for ways to compensate for the increased costs through substitution and innovation.

Taxes distort the behavior of individuals, families, and businesses. Individuals and firms make decisions based on prices. Taxes change the relative prices of goods, services, and inputs by making some inputs more expensive and others relatively less expensive. This distorts firms' decisions about what to produce and how, where, and when to produce it. Taxes can also reduce the after-tax income that workers get from working or taking advanced training or education and the net returns that investors get from employing their capital in one industry rather than another. This chapter reviews the extensive evidence from economic research on the impact of taxes on our decisions to work more, save, invest, and engage in entrepreneurial activity.

Organization

Section 1 defines a key concept in the discussion of taxes: marginal tax rates. Section 2 discusses the impact of taxes on economic growth. Section 3 reviews evidence on the impact of taxes on labor supply. Section 4 examines taxes and investment. Section 5 presents the impact of taxes on entrepreneurship and risk-taking.

1 ◈ Marginal tax rates

Most research on taxes focuses on marginal tax rates. A marginal tax rate (MTR) refers to the tax rate that applies to the next dollar of income earned. MTRs directly affect the proportion of increased income that is left after taxes and is therefore a critical determinant of economic behavior. In other words, when deciding whether or not to work an additional hour, to improve one's skills through education, to save, or to invest, the tax rate most important to an individual or business is the MTR (Chen, 2000). The higher the MTR, the lower the return to productive activity, and thus the reduced incentives for individuals, families, or businesses to work, save, invest, and engage in entrepreneurship.

Although this chapter primarily focuses on the impact of marginal tax rates on economic behavior, another important concept in the analysis of taxes is the average tax rate (ATR). The ATR refers to total taxes paid as a proportion of total taxable income for a given period: the ATR reflects the average tax burden faced by an individual, household, or firm. The ATR, like the MTR, can influence economic well-being. For example, when government is larger (that is, government spends more relative to the total economy), individuals face higher average tax burdens, which can translate into lower economic performance.

2 ◈ Taxes and economic growth

Economic growth is a widely used indicator of an economy's health. It is measured by the annual percentage change in a nation's gross domestic product (GDP).[1] Since taxes affect the returns of working, saving, investing, and entrepreneurship, they ultimately have an impact on the growth rate of the overall economy. This is true especially of high marginal taxes. Section 2 reviews the existing research on taxes and economic growth, examining tax rates, tax structure (or tax mix), and the degree of progressivity.[2]

Tax rates

There is a large body of scholarly research that supports the argument that high marginal tax rates reduce economic growth. Two studies completed by the European scholars Fabio Padovano and Emma Galli (2001; 2002) confirm the negative effects of high marginal tax rates on economic growth. Using data for 23 OECD countries from 1951 to 1990, Padovano and Galli (2001) found that high marginal tax rates and progressivity tended to be negatively associated with long-term economic growth. They followed up their original study in 2002 and found that an increase of 10 percentage points in marginal tax rates decreased the annual rate of economic growth by 0.23 percentage points.

A number of additional studies corroborate the finding that high and increasing marginal taxes negatively affect economic growth. For example, Reinhard Koester and Roger Kormendi (1989), using data for 63 countries during the 1970s, found that reducing the progressivity of the tax system while allowing the government the same tax revenue as a percentage of GDP led to higher levels of national income. Similarly, Professors John Mullen and Martin Williams (1994), using US state data from 1969 to 1986, examined the impact of state and local tax structures on the economic performance of states. The authors concluded that "lowering marginal tax rates can have a considerable positive impact on growth" and that "creating a less confiscatory tax structure, while maintaining the same average

---

1 ❖ GDP is the market value of all goods and services produced within a jurisdiction during a certain period.

2 ❖ "Progressivity" refers to a structure of tax rates in which income-tax rates increase as an individual earns more income.

level of taxation, enables sub-national governments to spur economic growth" (Mullen and Williams, 1994: 703).[3]

Yet another study by Eric Engen and Jonathan Skinner (1996) examined more than 20 studies looking at evidence on tax rates and economic growth in the United States and abroad. They concluded from their review of these studies that "a major tax reform reducing all marginal rates by 5 percentage points, and average tax rates by 2.5 percentage points, is predicted to increase long-term growth rates by between 0.2 and 0.3 percentage points" (Engen and Skinner 1996: 34).[4]

Francesco Daveri and Guido Tabellini (2000) argued that the slowing of economic growth in Europe in the post-war period was caused by a rapid growth in labor costs. European labor costs had gone up because of higher taxes on labor income, among other reasons. Using a panel of 14 OECD countries over the period from 1965 to 1995, they estimated that an increase of 14 percentage points in labor income-tax rates in continental European Union (EU) countries could account for a reduction in economic growth of 0.4 percentage points per year.[5]

Most recently, American professors Christina and David Romer (2007) analyzed the impact of changes in the level of taxation on promoting economic growth. In this important study, the authors investigated the effects of tax reforms on GDP in the United States in the post-war period. The study found that such tax changes had very large effects on GDP: a tax increase of 1% of GDP lowered output as measured by real GDP by roughly 2% to 3%. They also found that tax increases led to sharp falls in investment. which ultimately depressed GDP.

---

3 ◆ Becsi (1996), using US state data for the period from 1960 to 1992, confirmed this result: higher marginal tax rates were associated with lower economic growth.

4 ◆ While this may appear small, the cumulative effective can be enormous. The authors speculated that, if an inefficient tax structure had been in place in the US from 1960 to 1996, the amount of output currently lost would have totalled more than $500 billion annually or 6.4% of 1996 GDP.

5 ◆ Daveri and Tabellini also found that the increase in labor income-tax rates caused a rise in unemployment. Specifically, an increase of 14 percentage points in labor income-tax rates accounted for a rise in unemployment of roughly 4 percentage points.

Tax structure

Tax structure refers to the "mix" of taxes on physical capital, income, wages, and consumption levied by governments. In other words, it indicates how much of the total tax revenue is collected from each type of tax. The choice of tax mix is important since some taxes (such as taxes on income) appear to be more damaging to the economy than others (like taxes on goods and services).[6]

Several studies found evidence that tax structure affects economic growth. For example, Richard Kneller and his colleagues (1999), using data for 22 OECD countries from 1970 to 1995, found that what are considered distortionary taxes (i.e. taxes on income, profit, payroll, and property as well as social security contributions) reduced growth, while non-distortionary taxes (i.e. taxes on domestic goods and services) did not. Specifically, their more conservative estimates suggested that reducing distortionary taxes by 1% of GDP would increase the growth rate by between 0.1% and 0.2% per year. Another study, by Frida Widmalm (2001), examined the relationship between taxation and economic growth in 23 OECD countries for the period from 1965 to 1990. The author argued that certain tax mixes had an adverse impact on growth. Specifically, Widmalm found that there was a negative relationship between the share of total taxes levied on personal income and economic growth.

Recently, economists Young Lee and Roger Gordon (2005) explored the influence of corporate (business) taxes on economic growth. Using data for 70 countries for the period from 1970 to 1997, they found that increases in corporate tax rates led to lower growth rates within countries over time. In fact, their analysis suggested that a reduction of 10 percentage points in corporate taxes would raise the annual growth rate of countries by one to two percentage points.[7]

---

6 ◆ See Clemens et al. (2007) for a comprehensive discussion about the economic cost of different types of taxes.

7 ◆ Results would vary depending on the variables included in the analysis. In their estimation, the authors also considered other variables that could affect economic growth besides corporate tax rates, such as personal and commodity tax rates, population growth rates, inflation rate, and trade openness. When only

Tax progressivity

Several studies have evaluated the effects upon economic growth of tax progressivity, which has traditionally been achieved by applying higher tax rates to higher income groups. These studies have examined the impact of shifting from a tax system with a rising MTR to a flat-tax system.[8] A tax system with a rising MTR uses tax brackets to classify incomes, with higher income brackets taxed at higher rates. On the other hand, a flat tax is essentially a tax with a constant marginal tax rate levied on both household and business income.[9]

A paper by Elizabeth Caucutt and colleagues (2000), using data for the US economy, found that changes in the progressivity of tax rates can have important effects on growth. In particular, they found that a tax system with a rising MTR reduced growth by 0.13 to 0.53 percentage points.[10] Similarly, Stephen Cassou and Kevin Lansing (2004) assessed the growth effects of shifting from a system with a rising MTR to a flat tax. The authors predicted that a shift to a flat-tax

---

corporate tax rates are considered in the estimation, results show that a 10 percentage point increase in corporate tax rates is associated with a 0.64 percentage point increase in the annual growth rate of GDP per capita.

8 ◆ Both these tax systems are classified as "progressive tax systems," defined as tax systems that take a greater proportion of income from those with high incomes than from those with low incomes. A progressive tax system achieves vertical equity in one of two ways. Vertical equity refers to a method of collecting income tax in which the amount of taxes paid increases with the amount of income earned. The tax systems of most countries use rising MTRs to achieve vertical equity. The alternative means of achieving vertical equity is through a system of proportional tax (like the flat-tax system) in which the proportion of taxes paid increases with income, e.g. a 10% increase in income causes a 10% increase in taxes paid.

9 ◆ The flat tax can eliminate the negative effects of high and increasing marginal tax rates while maintaining progressivity. Progressivity within a system based on a flat tax or a single-rate tax is achieved through a low-income exemption. Individuals, families, and businesses continue to pay more tax as they earn more but no longer face increasing marginal tax rates. Thus, the flat tax system achieves progressivity while avoiding negative effects associated with high and increasing marginal tax rates.

10 ◆ Widmalm (2001) also found that tax progressivity was also associated with low economic growth.

system without changing the amount of tax revenue collected could permanently increase per-capita growth by 0.009 to 0.143 percentage points per year relative to a progressive tax system.[11]

3 ◆ Taxes and labor supply

Taxes are an important determinant of labor supply. By changing the returns (after-tax wage) to employment, taxes influence the number of hours workers are willing to work. They also influence unemployed workers' decision to join the workforce. High taxes reduce work effort and discourage entry into the labor market.

Numerous academic studies provide compelling evidence that taxes reduce labor supply, both in terms of hours worked and participation in the workforce.[12] An important contribution to the international research in this area was recently made by Edward Prescott (2004). Prescott examined the role of marginal tax rates in accounting for changes in hours worked and employment income for the working age population (15 to 64 years) in the G-7 countries for the periods from 1970 to 1974 and 1993 to 1996.[13] The author found that differences in marginal tax rates accounted for a large part of the differences in hours worked in the early 1970s and the early 1990s in the United States and several European countries. Specifically, lower marginal tax rates largely accounted for the fact that Americans now work nearly 50% more than the Germans, the French, and the Italians compared to the early 1970s.

Similarly, Steven J. Davis and Magnus Henrekson (2004) recently completed a study investigating the effects of national differences in tax

---

11 ◆ For further research that examines the quantitative effects of tax reform on long-run growth, see King and Rebelo, 1990; Rebelo, 1991; Devereux and Love, 1994; and Milesi-Ferreti et al., 1998.

12 ◆ See Feldstein, 2006 for a non-technical discussion of marginal tax rates and labor supply.

13 ◆ The author only considered hours worked in the taxed market sector. Paid vacations, sick leave, and holidays and time spent working in the underground economy or in the home sector were not counted.

rates on employment income, payrolls, and consumer spending. The authors posited that higher tax rates reduce the reward to work and thus, decrease work time in the private sector and increase the size of the underground economy.[14] After examining data from 16 industrialized countries during the 1990s, they found that a tax rate increase of 12.8 percentage points led to 122 fewer hours worked per adult per year, which translated to a decline of 4.9 percentage points in total employment and an increase in the underground economy of roughly 3.8% of GDP.

A study by Emanuela Cardia and colleagues (2003) supported these findings. The authors analyzed the impact of changes in labor-tax rates on hours worked across several countries, including Canada and the United States. They found that a decrease of 10 percentage points in marginal tax rates increased the weekly hours worked by between 4.5% (in Germany) and 18.0% (in the United States). Weekly hours worked increased by 9.9% in Canada; the range in the United States was from 12.8% to 18.0%, depending on the period analyzed.

In a more recent study, Lee Ohanian and colleagues (2006) explained trends in average hours worked by the working age population (15 to 64 years) across 21 OECD countries from 1956 to 2004. While there is considerable variation in trends across countries, average hours worked has fallen substantially in most OECD countries over the period: average hours worked by the working population in 2004 were almost 20% below their 1956 levels. The authors found that income and consumption taxes better explained the decrease in hours worked than other policy factors such as labor regulations, trade-union membership, collective bargaining, and the size and duration of unemployment benefits. These findings strongly suggest that taxes can account for most of the changes in hours worked both over time and across countries.

Several studies have investigated the impact of taxes on labor supply in the context of tax reforms in the United States. A key contributor

---

14 ◆ The underground economy refers to non-market activities undertaken by individuals to avoid paying taxes. An increase in taxes would encourage market participants to channel their efforts away from productive but taxed activities to less productive but untaxed activities.

in this area is Harvard Professor Martin Feldstein. In a study published in the *American Economic Review,* Feldstein (1995a) reviewed all of the major literature available on the impact of the Tax Reform Act of 1986 on labor supply in the United States. The consensus in the existing research was that men's working hours and participation rates were generally insensitive to net wages (after-tax wages) but that married women's working hours and participation rates were substantially more sensitive. He further noted that it was wrong to say that taxes did not affect the supply of men's labor since the amount of "labor" also depended on the intensity of work effort, the nature of the occupation, on-the-job acquisition of skills, and many other dimensions, all of which can be influenced by changes in tax rates (Feldstein, 1995b).

Similarly, Nada Eissa and colleagues (2004) examined the impact of four major changes in US federal tax policy passed in 1986, 1990, 1993, and 2001 on hours worked and participation in the labor force by single mothers. These policy changes created substantial benefits for lower-income taxpayers through reduced marginal tax rates and increased personal exemptions and deductions. The authors found that all four tax reforms reduced the tax burden on low-income single mothers and increased both hours worked and employment. The benefits of the 1986 reform were especially large, creating a 7.94% reduction in the tax burden and an efficiency gain[15] of 7.09% of employment income. The authors also found that most of the efficiency gains from the tax reforms were from increased employment.[16]

Most recently, Ziliak and Kniesner (2005) used the US tax reforms of the 1980s and 1990s to examine the impact of income taxes on labor supply. Using data on male household heads from 1980 to 1999, the authors found that a 10% increase in net wages (after-tax wages)

---

15 ◆ An efficiency gain from a tax reform results when some of the distortions in behavior as a result of taxes are reduced. For instance, a reduction in marginal tax rates on income would encourage more people to enter the workforce in addition to increasing hours worked.

16 ◆ In fact, while increased employment accounted for over three quarters of the efficiency gain from the 1986 tax reform, it accounted for essentially all of the gain from the 1990 reform.

increased hours worked by 3%.[17] The authors also estimated that the efficiency cost[18] of an additional dollar of tax in the regimes prior to the reforms was 16% to 21%.[19]

There is also evidence from European countries that tax rates influence labor supply. For example, Richard Blundell and colleagues (1998) examined changes in the United Kingdom's tax policy from 1978 to 1992 and the impact of those changes on labor supply. They concluded that increases in after-tax wage rates had a positive impact on hours worked.

More recently, Anders Klevmarken (2000) provided corroborating evidence from Sweden. Using longitudinal data covering the period after the Swedish tax reform of 1991 that saw reductions in marginal tax rates, he concluded that working women increased their hours worked by approximately 10%.[20]

---

17 ◆ Earlier, Bosworth and Burtless (1992), examining the effects of the Tax Reform Act of 1986 and the 1981 tax cuts in the United States on labor supply, found that average hours worked among adult women accelerated in the 1980s and average hours worked among adult men stabilized or rose slowly after a long period of decline after 1981. Additionally, increases in hours worked were also apparent among earners in affluent families and especially married women in those families. Similarly, Eissa (1995) examined the labor supply of high-income, married women before and after 1986. She found that women from high-income families adjusted their work to take more advantage of increased after-tax incomes available after the reform.

18 ◆ The efficiency costs of a tax go beyond the amount of tax collected. They emerge because taxes distort the decisions of individuals, families, and businesses to engage in productive activities (working, spending, saving, and investing) by changing the relative prices of goods, services, and inputs, and by reducing incomes and returns to investment. A key method for quantifying these costs is referred to as the marginal efficiency cost (MEC). It calculates the cost of raising one additional dollar of tax revenue using different types of taxes. For a detailed discussion on efficiency costs of taxes, see Clemens et al., 2007.

19 ◆ Similar results were obtained by Ziliak and Kniesner (1999). Using panel data between 1978 and 1987, the authors concluded that the large-scale reductions in marginal tax rates increased men's labor supply by about 3% and reduced efficiency costs by about 16%.

20 ◆ For additional studies on Sweden, see Aronsson and Palme, 1998; Sundstrom, 1991; and Stuart, 1981.

There is also research examining the impact of tax rates on the labor supply of specific groups of workers. For instance, an interesting analysis by Norman Thurston (2002) provided some insights into how highly-paid professionals (specifically, physicians) reacted to changes in the tax rate. Using responses from the Robert Johnson Foundation's *Young Physicians Survey* (1987, 1991), the author found that physicians in states with higher taxes were likely to work fewer hours and more likely to control their work schedule than those in states with lower taxes. He also found that physicians in more highly taxed states were more likely to miss work due to illness or vacation (see also Thurston and Libby, 2000).

4 ◆ Taxes and investment

The level and structure of taxation imposed by governments are key determinants of the level of business investment. High business taxes reduce the after-tax rate of return on investment and thus reduce the amount of money that firms will reinvest in machinery, equipment and technology that make workers more productive. Section 4 reviews the existing research on taxes and investment, considering business taxes and investment; tax-deferred savings and investment income; and, capital gains tax.

Business taxes and investment
Investment is important for a nation's future well being. High marginal tax rates lower an investor's willingness to invest by lowering returns to investment.[21] A reduced amount of investment has a number of negative consequences including decreased productivity of workers and reduced output, employment, and ultimately, living standards.

---

21 ◆ In addition, taxes have the potential to affect investment spending through their impact on the cost of capital. For further details, see Chirinko and Meyer, 1997; Chirinko et al., 1999; Milligan et al., 1999; Cummins, 1998; and McKenzie and Thompson, 1997. A comprehensive review of investment and the cost of capital is available in Veldhuis and Clemens, 2006.

One of the most influential studies on the relationship between business taxes and investment was that by Robert Hall and Dale W. Jorgenson (1967) published in the *American Economic Review*. The authors calculated the effects of changes in tax policy on investment behavior for three major tax revisions after the Second World War in the United States.[22] They found that tax policy was highly effective in changing the level and timing of investment expenditures. They also found that tax policy had important effects on the composition of investment.[23]

Steven R. Fazzari, R. Glenn Hubbard, and Bruce Petersen (1988) analyzed the effects of taxes on capital spending. The authors investigated whether marginal or average tax rates had an impact on capital investment made by firms. They found for firms facing financing constraints,[24] the average tax rate was more important in determining investment than the marginal tax rate. In other words, lower average tax rates increased the amount of earnings firms have for reinvestment in capital. In addition, the authors noted that the elimination of corporate income taxes would increase investment by firms facing financing constraints. On the other hand, the authors argued that marginal tax rates were more important in influencing investment decisions for firms that did not face financing constraints. For such firms, lower

---

22 ◆ (1) The adoption of accelerated methods for computing depreciation for tax purposes in 1954; (2) the reduction of lifetimes used for calculating depreciation on equipment and machinery in 1962; (3) the investment tax credit for machinery and equipment of 1962.

23 ◆ According to their estimates, the liberalization of depreciation rules in 1954 resulted in a substantial shift from equipment to structures. On the other hand, the investment tax credit and depreciation guidelines of 1962 caused a shift toward equipment.

24 ◆ Financing constraints refer to limits on the ability of firms to use external funds (equity and debt) to finance their capital investments. Small or less established firms and firms operating in industries with new technology are more likely to face such constraints. Firms facing financing constraints usually rely on internal funds (profits) to finance investment.

marginal tax rates reduced the cost of new investment and stimulated capital investment.

Peter Clark (1993) investigated the behavior of businesses as regards equipment investment in the United States from 1953 to 1992. Clark estimated that a 1% increase in taxes would decrease equipment investment by 0.40%. In addition, a series of papers by Jason Cummins, Kevin Hasset, and Glenn Hubbard provided empirical evidence on the influence of business taxes on capital investment. First, their 1994 study used US tax reforms as natural experiments to estimate the responsiveness of investment in fixed assets. The authors concluded that investment changed significantly and in a manner consistent with the tax changes subsequent to every major business tax reform since 1962. Further, investment spending was most responsive in firms facing the greatest change in tax incentives.

A subsequent paper by Cummins and colleagues (1996) investigated the impact of tax reforms on investment using a cross-country comparison. The authors examined the impact of tax reforms on the investment decisions of over 3,000 firms from 1981 to 1992 in 14 countries, including Canada, that were members of the OECD. The authors found that changes in tax policy did indeed affect investment levels in 12 of the 14 countries, including Canada.[25]

Another paper, by Robert Carroll and colleagues (1998), found that "a 5 percentage point rise in marginal tax rates would reduce the proportion of entrepreneurs who make new capital investment by 10.4%. Further, such a tax increase would lower average capital investment by 9.9%" (1998: 2). Finally, Gustavo Ventura (1999) modeled the effects of a broad-based flat-tax reform such as that proposed by Professors Hall and Rabushka in their publication, *The Flat Tax* (1985).[26] Ventura concluded that the elimination of taxes on capital did indeed have a positive effect on capital accumulation and labor supply.

---

25 ◆ In the other two countries, changes in tax policy did not have any effect on investment levels.

26 ◆ For a discussion of Hall and Rabushka's flat-tax proposal, see Clemens and Emes, 2001.

Tax-deferred savings and investment income

An interesting, though indirect, method of determining whether or not marginal tax rates affect behavior is to question whether tax-deferred savings accounts are affected by marginal tax rates. The theory is that the more tax one must pay on an additional dollar of income (higher marginal rate), the greater incentive one has to reduce the portion of the dollar that is subject to tax.[27] For example, investing in Registered Retirement Savings Plans (RRSPs) in Canada or Individual Retirement Accounts (IRAs) in the United States would reduce the portion of additional income subject to income tax. In fact, in an important study, Kevin Milligan (2002) found that an increase of 10 percentage points in the marginal tax rate (MTR) increased the probability of participation in tax-deferred accounts, specifically RRSPs, by 8%. At the same time, Eaton (2002) found that a one-percentage point increase in tax rates would increase the likelihood of participation in IRAs between 2% and 3%.

Several other studies also corroborate these findings. Cherie O'Neil and Rodney Thompson (1987) analyzed the influence of the Tax Reform Act of 1986 (TRA86) on IRAs using sample data from the Internal Revenue Agency for the period from 1979 to 1982. Their analysis concluded that the decision to contribute to an IRA depended on the individual's marginal tax rate, the presence of interest income, the filing status of the taxpayer, and geographic location. Results showed that both the MTR and presence of interest income had a significant and positive influence on the decision to participate in an IRA.[28] Specific results regarding MTRs revealed that a decrease of one percentage point in the MTR was associated with a 0.5% to 1% decrease in the probability of participation.[29] Similarly, David Joulfaian and David Richardson (2001)

---

27 ◆ Although not discussed here, marginal tax rates also influence the portfolio composition of investments. For further details, see Feldstein, 1976 and Hubbard, 1985.

28 ◆ Results show additionally that single people participate less in IRA contributions.

29 ◆ This study was later updated by Long (1988) who found that the influence of the Tax Reform Act of 1986 on IRAs was smaller than originally determined, but still positive and significant.

found that higher MTRs tended to increase the probability of participation in tax-deferred retirement savings plans in the United States.

A related issue is the impact of taxes on investment income. Raj Chetty and Emmanuel Saez (2004) examined the effect of the 2003 dividend tax cut in the United States, which lowered the individual income-tax burden on dividends from a maximum rate of 35% to 15%. Using data from 1980 to 2004, the authors found a sharp and widespread surge in dividend payments by firms following the tax cut. Specifically, the fraction of publicly traded firms[30] paying dividends increased in 2003 after having declined continuously for more than two decades. Most firms also initiated regular dividend payments as opposed to special one-time payments and significantly raised the amounts of dividend payments made. Overall, the authors estimated that total dividends paid by firms increased by 20% within six quarters (1½ years) after the reform. The observed effects were consistent across firm sizes, providing clear evidence of the impact of dividend taxes on the magnitude and frequency of dividend payments.[31]

Capital gains tax

Taxes on capital gains raise revenues for the government but also impose economic costs that exceed the amount of tax collected.[32] The additional cost is incurred because individuals and businesses alter their behavior when the tax reduces the returns on their investments. As a result, capital gains taxes have a substantial impact on the reallocation of capital, the stock of capital, and the level of entrepreneurship in Canada.[33]

Capital gains taxes significantly impede the reallocation of capital from older, less profitable, investments to those with higher rates of return. Several studies have investigated the impact of capital gains

---

30 ◆ The firms analyzed in the study exclude those in the financial and utility sectors.

31 ◆ For related studies, see Chetty and Saez, 2004, 2006.

32 ◆ See Veldhuis et al., 2007 for a more detailed discussion of the economic costs of capital gains taxes.

33 ◆ See section 5, Taxes, entrepreneurship, and risk-taking for further details on the impact of capital gains taxes on entrepreneurship.

taxes on the reallocation of capital, or what economists call the "lock-in effect."[34] For example, an influential paper by Harvard Professor Martin Feldstein and his colleagues Joel Slemrod and Shlomo Yitzhaki (1980) was one of the first to provide an empirical analysis of the effect of taxation on the realization of capital gains (sale of corporate stocks at a profit). The authors found a significant lock-in effect: an increase of 10 percentage points in the marginal tax rate reduced the probability of selling a stock by 6.5 percentage points.

In another related study, Paul Bolster, Lawrence Lindsey, and Andrew Mitrusi (1989) evaluated the impact of the elimination in 1986 of favorable tax treatments of long-term capital gains on stock market activity in the United States.[35] The authors examined trading volume on the New York Stock Exchange (NYSE) and the American Stock and Options Exchange (AMEX) from 1976 to 1987. They found that trading volume increased significantly in the months leading up to the change and declined significantly after favorable treatment of capital gains was eliminated: trading volume was 15% lower in the January of 1987 compared to previous Januaries in the period analyzed. The empirical results suggested that the expected increase in the tax rate on capital gains encouraged investors to reallocate capital prior to the change.

5 ◈ Taxes, entrepreneurship and risk-taking

Entrepreneurship is widely recognized as a critical determinant of growth-enhancing activities such as job creation, innovation, and productivity gains. Taxes can have an influential impact on

---

34 ◆ Many studies provide empirical evidence of the existence of a lock-in effect. For instance, Jog (1995) finds evidence of a lock-in effect in Canada by examining the change in capital-gains realizations after the 1985 introduction of a capital-gains exemption. Also, see Landsman and Shackelford, 1995; Shackelford, 2000; Blouin et al., 2000; and Dai et al., 2006 for empirical evidence of the lock-in effect.

35 ◆ Prior to 1987, capital gains on financial assets held for at least six months were generally taxed at 40% of the tax rate applied to other sources of income. As of January 1987, however, most financial assets were taxed at the same rate as other income sources.

entrepreneurship and risk-taking by serving to encourage or deter such activity. This section reviews the large and growing body of research on the impact of taxes and its structure on entrepreneurship.

Economists William Gentry and Glenn Hubbard (2000) analyzed the impact of tax progressivity on the decision to become an entrepreneur (defined as self-employed) using American data over the period from 1979 to 1992. The authors found evidence that a more progressive tax structure reduced the probability of entering self-employment since, if tax rates are more progressive, entrepreneurs pay substantial taxes on profits earned but save little through taxes reduced by writing off losses incurred. In other words, there is a tax on "success" that discourages entry.[36]

Research also shows that taxes can affect the growth of small entrepreneurial businesses. For example, a series of papers by Robert Carroll and his colleagues provided empirical evidence on the influence of taxes on the growth of small firms. Their first paper (2000) studied the effect of entrepreneurs' personal income-tax rates on their use of hired labor. Using tax returns of sole proprietors before and after the US Tax Reform Act of 1986,[37] the authors found that personal income taxes exert a significant influence on the probability of hiring workers. Specifically, increasing the entrepreneur's "tax price" (one minus the marginal tax rate)[38] by 10% raised the mean probability of hiring by about 12%.

Similarly, a subsequent paper (Carroll et al., 2001), also using data from tax returns between 1985 and 1988, found that an increase in a sole proprietor's tax price (one minus the marginal tax rate) increased the

---

36 ◆ A more recent study by Gentry and Hubbard (2004) explored the role of tax policy on entrepreneurship as measured by self-employment. The authors found that the level of the marginal tax rate and the progressivity of the tax discouraged entrepreneurship, and significantly so for some groups of households.

37 ◆ The Tax Reform Act of 1986 dramatically reduced marginal personal income-tax rates.

38 ◆ The "tax price" represents the proportion of a dollar of profits earned by an entrepreneur after taxes. A higher tax price (resulting from a lower tax rate) implies that entrepreneurs keep a higher proportion of a dollar of profits after tax.

size of his or her business.[39] Specifically, raising the sole proprietor's tax price by 10% increased revenues by about 8.4%. The authors also concluded that a decrease in the marginal tax rate levied on a sole proprietor from 50% to 33% would lead to an increase in receipts (revenues) of about 28%.

Most recently, Julie Cullen and Roger Gordon (2007) analyzed the extent to which the tax system affects the amount of entrepreneurial risk-taking. The authors measured risk-taking as the business losses that occur when an entrepreneur's business has expenses that exceed revenues (on a yearly basis). Higher business losses indicate that entrepreneurs are taking more risks to bring new ideas (i.e. goods and services) to market. Using a sample of American personal income-tax returns from 1964 to 1993, the authors found that taxes did influence entrepreneurial risk-taking but their impact differed according to the type of tax. Overall, the authors estimated that a reduction in personal tax rates of 5 percentage points (in every income bracket) lead to a 40% decrease in entrepreneurial risk-taking since lower personal tax rates reduce the amount of business loss entrepreneurs can deduct from taxable income. On the other hand, several tax changes increased entrepreneurial risk-taking. For instance, the authors found that a shift to a 20% flat tax increased entrepreneurial activity by 15% to 20%. Introducing a negative income tax, whereby any negative taxable income generates a tax refund, more than doubles the amount of entrepreneurial risk taking. Allowing people to deduct business losses on their personal income-tax return would increase entrepreneurial risk taking by 50% to 100%. A reduction in capital gains taxes also increased entrepreneurial risk-taking.

Personal income tax and payroll taxes are not the only classes of tax that affect entrepreneurial activity. Capital gains taxes also have a detrimental impact on entrepreneurship since they reduce the return that entrepreneurs, venture capitalists, and other investors receive from risk-taking, innovation, and work effort. An expectation of lower returns decreases the number of entrepreneurs and risk-

---

39 ◆ In other words, a lower marginal tax rate stimulated business growth among sole proprietors.

takers and ultimately reduces investment, technological advances, employment, and overall economic growth.

A large body of academic research has investigated the impact of capital gains taxes on entrepreneurship. A seminal study by Professor James Poterba (1989) provided the theoretical framework for examining the impact of capital-gains tax policy on entrepreneurship. Poterba highlighted that potential entrepreneurs compared the compensation obtained from employment at an established firm with the expected payoff from a start-up where a larger share of their compensation would consist of a capital gain.[40] The author concluded that a reduction in the capital gains tax raises the attractiveness of becoming an entrepreneur and is likely to increase the demand for venture capital, a key source of funding for new entrepreneurial businesses.

Paul Gompers and Josh Lerner (1998) tested Poterba's argument by exploring the key drivers of venture capital funding. Analyzing the stock of venture capital and tax rates on capital gains from 1972 to 1994, Gompers and Lerner found that an increase of one percentage-point in the rate of capital gains tax was associated with a 3.8% reduction in venture capital funding.

More recently, a study by Christian Keuschnigg and Soren Bo Nielsen (2004) investigated the impact that taxes and other public policies (i.e. subsidies to support new firms) had on the creation and success of businesses that were financed by venture capital. Keuschnigg and Nielsen found that "even a small capital gains tax ... diminishes incentives to provide entrepreneurial effort" (2004: 1033). Similarly, Donald Bruce and Mohammed Mohsin (2006) presented an empirical analysis of tax policy and entrepreneurship in the United States. The authors examined personal income-tax rates, capital gains taxes, and corporate income-tax rates on self-employment rates (a proxy for entrepreneurship). The authors found that a reduction of one percentage point in the capital-gains tax rate was associated with an increase of from 0.11 to 0.15 percentage point in self-employment rates.

---

40 ◆ A capital gain (or loss) generally refers to the price of an asset when it is sold compared to its purchase price. A capital gain occurs if the value of the asset at the time of sale is greater than the original purchase price.

More generally, Marco Da Rin and colleagues (2006) examined the impact of a number of government policies on new ventures (start-up businesses) in 14 European countries from 1988 to 2001. The authors used two measures to determine whether policies were successful: the proportion of high-technology investments to total venture investments (high-tech ratio) and the proportion of early-stage investments to total venture investments (early-stage ratio). They concluded that reducing capital gains tax, opening a new venture stock market, and reducing labor regulations were the three policies that worked well to increase the proportion of high-tech and early-stage ventures.

Conclusion

The evidence from economic research indicates that tax rates—and in particular marginal tax rates—do indeed influence individual behavior when it comes to working, investing, saving and entrepreneurship. Perhaps most important is the insight that high and increasing marginal taxes contribute to lower rates of economic growth, reduced rates of personal income growth, lower rates of capital formation, lower than expected aggregate labor supply, and reduced entrepreneurship. In short, high and increasing marginal tax rates reduce economic growth by creating strong disincentives to hard work, savings, investment, and entrepreneurship.

References

Aronsson, Thomas, and Marten Palme (1998). A Decade of Tax and Benefit Reforms in Sweden: Effects on Labour Supply, Welfare and Inequality. *Economica* 65: 39–67.

Becsi, Zsolt (1996). Do State and Local Taxes Affect Relative State Growth? *Economic Review* 81, 2 (March/April): 18–36. Federal Reserve Bank of Atlanta.

Blouin, Jennifer, Jana Smith Raedy, and Douglas Shackelford (2000). *Capital Gains Holding Periods and Equity Trading: Evidence from the 1998 Act.* NBER working paper 7827. National Bureau of Economic Research.

Blundell, Richard, Alan Duncan, and Costas Meghir (1998). Estimating Labor Supply Responses Using Tax Reforms. *Econometrica* 66, 4 (July): 827–61.

Bolster, Paul, Lawrence Lindsey, and Andrew Mitrusi (1989). Tax-Induced Trading: The Effect of the 1986 Tax Reform Act on Stock Market Activity. *Journal of Finance* 44, 2 (June): 327–44.

Bosworth, B., and G. Burtless (1992). Effects of Tax Reform on Labour Supply, Investment and Saving. *Journal of Economic Perspectives* 6, 1: 3–25.

Bruce, Donald, and Mohammed Mohsin (2006). Tax Policy and Entrepreneurship: New Times Series Evidence. *Small Business Economics* 26: 409–25.

Cardia, Emanuela, Norma Kozhaya, and Francisco J. Ruge-Murcia (2003). Distortionary Taxation and Labour Supply. *Journal of Money, Credit, and Banking* 35, 3 (June): 350–73.

Carroll, Robert, Douglas Holtz-Eakin, Mark Rider, and Harvey S. Rosen (1998). *Entrepreneurs, Income Taxes, and Investment.* NBER working paper 6374 (January). National Bureau of Economic Research.

Carroll, Robert, Douglas Holtz-Eakin, Mark Rider, and Harvey S. Rosen (2000). Income Taxes and Entrepreneurs' Use of Labor. *Journal of Labor Economics* 18, 2 (April): 324–51.

Carroll, Robert, Douglas Holtz-Eakin, Mark Rider, and Harvey S. Rosen (2001). Personal Income Taxes and the Growth of Small Firms. In J. Poterba, ed., *Tax Policy and the Economy* (MIT Press): 121–47.

Cassou, Stephen, and Kevin Lansing (2004). Growth Effects of Shifting from a Graduated-Rate Tax System to a Flat Tax. *Economic Inquiry* 42, 2 (April): 194–213.

Caucutt, Elizabeth M., Selahattin Imrohoroglu, and Krishan B. Kumar (2000). *Does the Progressivity of Taxes Matter for Economic Growth?* Discussion Paper 138. Institute for Empirical Macroeconomics, Federal Reserve Bank of Minneapolis.

Chen, Duanjie (2000). *The Marginal Effective Tax Rate: The Only Tax Rate that Matters in Capital Allocation.* CD Howe Institute.

Chetty, Raj, and Emmanuel Saez (2004). *Do Dividend Payments Respond to Taxes? Preliminary Evidence from the 2003 Dividend Tax Cut.* NBER Working Paper 10572. National Bureau of Economic Research.

Chirinko, Robert, and Andrew Meyer (1997). The User Cost of Capital and Investment Spending: Implications for Canadian Firms. In Paul J. N. Halpern, ed., *Financing Growth in Canada* (University of Calgary Press): 17–69.

Chirinko, Robert, Steven M. Fazzari, and Andrew P. Meyer (1999). How Responsive Is Business Capital Formation to Its User Cost? An Exploration with Micro Data. *Journal of Public Economics* 74: 53–80.

Clark, Peter (1993). Tax Incentives and Equipment Investment. *Brookings Papers on Economic Activity 1993:1, Macroeconomics*: 317–39.

Clemens, Jason, and Joel Emes (2001). *Flat Tax: Issues and Principles*. Critical Issues Bulletin. The Fraser Institute.

Clemens, Jason, Niels Veldhuis, and Milagros Palacios (2007). *Tax Efficiency: Not All Taxes Are Created Equal*. Studies in Economic Prosperity No. 4. The Fraser Institute.

Cullen, Julie, and Roger Gordon (2007). Taxes and Entrepreneurial Risk-taking: Theory and Evidence for the U.S. *Journal of Public Economics* 91: 1479–505.

Cummins, Jason (1998). *Taxation and the Sources of Growth: Estimates from United States Multinational Corporations*. NBER working paper 6533. National Bureau of Economic Research.

Cummins, Jason G., Kevin A. Hassett, and R. Glenn Hubbard (1994). A Reconsideration of Investment Behavior Using Tax Reforms as Natural Experiments. *Brookings Papers on Economic Activity 1994:2 Macroeconomics*: 1–74.

Cummins, Jason, Kevin Hassett, and Glen Hubbard (1996). Tax Reforms and Investment: A Cross-Country Comparison. *Journal of Public Economics* 62, 1–2: 237–73.

Dai, Zhonglan, Edward Maydew, Douglas Shackelford, and Harold Zhang (2006). *Capital Gains Taxes and Asset Prices: Capitalization or Lock-in?* NBER working paper 12342. National Bureau of Economic Research.

Da Rin, Marco, Giovanna Nicodano, and Alessandro Sembenelli (2006). Public Policy and the Creation of Active Venture Capital Markets. *Journal of Public Economics* 90, 8-9: 1699–723.

Daveri, Francesco, and Guido Tabellini (2000). Unemployment, growth and taxation in industrial countries. *Economic Policy* 15, 30: 47–104.

Davis, Steven J., and Magnus Henrekson (2004). *Tax Effects on Work Activity, Industry Mix and Shadow Economy Size: Evidence from Rich-Country Comparisons*. NBER working paper 10509. National Bureau of Economic Research.

Devereux, M.B., and D.R.F. Love (1994). The Effects of Factor Taxation in a Two-Sector Model of Endogenous Growth. *Canadian Journal of Economics* 27, 3: 509–36.

Domar, Evsey D., and Richard Musgrave (1944). Proportional Income taxation and Risk-taking. *Quarterly Journal of Economics* 58: 388–422.

Eaton, David H. (2002). The Impact of the Source of Changes in Marginal Tax Rates on Participation in Individual Retirement Accounts. *Journal of the American Taxation Association* 24, 1: 46–59.

Eissa, Nada (1995). *Taxation and Labor Supply of Married Women: The Tax Reform Act of the 1986 as a Natural Experiment*. NBER working paper 5023. National Bureau of Economic Research.

Eissa, Nada, Henrik J. Kleven and Claus T. Kreiner (2004). *Evaluation of Four Tax Reforms in the United States: Labor Supply and Welfare Effects for Single Mothers*. NBER working paper 10935. National Bureau of Economic Research.

Engen, Eric, and Jonathan Skinner (1996). Taxation and Economic Growth. *National Tax Journal* 49, 4 (December): 617–42.

Fazzari, Steven, R. Glenn Hubbard, and Bruce Petersen (1988). Investment, Financing Decisions, and Tax Policy. *American Economic Review* 78, 2: 200–05.

Feldstein, Martin (1976). Personal Taxation and Portfolio Composition: An Econometric Analysis. *Econometrica* 44, 4: 631–50.

Feldstein, Martin (1995a). Behavioral Responses to Tax Rates: Evidence from the Tax Reform Act of 1986. *American Economic Review* 85, 2: 170–74.

Feldstein, Martin (1995b). The Effect of Marginal Tax Rates on Taxable Income: A Panel Study of the 1986 Tax Reform Act. *Journal of Political Economy* 103, 3: 551–72.

Feldstein, Martin (2006). The Effect of Taxes on Efficiency and Growth. NBER working paper 12201. National Bureau of Economic Research.

Feldstein, Martin, Joel Slemrod, and Shlomo Yitzhaki (1980). The Effects of Taxation on the Selling of Corporate Stock and the Realization of Capital Gains. *Quarterly Journal of Economics* 94, 4: 777–91.

Gentry, William M., and R. Glenn Hubbard (2000). Tax Policy and Entrepreneurial Entry. *American Economic Review* 90, 2: 283–87.

Gentry, William M., and R. Glenn Hubbard (2004). *"Success Taxes," Entrepreneurial Entry, and Innovation*. NBER working paper 10551. National Bureau of Economic Research.

Gompers, Paul, and Josh Lerner (1998). What Drives Venture Capital Fundraising? *Brookings Papers on Economic Activity, Microeconomics: 1998*: 149–92.

Hall, Robert E. and Alvin Rabushka (1985). *The Flat Tax*. Hoover Institution Press.

Hall, Robert, and Dale W. Jorgenson (1967). Tax Policy and Investment Behavior. *American Economic Review* 57, 3: 391–414.

Hubbard, R. Glenn (1985). Personal Taxation, Pension Wealth, and Portfolio Composition. *Review of Economics and Statistics* 67, 1: 53–60.

Jog, Vijay (1995). The Lifetime Capital Gains Exemption: Corporate Financing, Risk-Taking and Allocation Efficiency. *Canadian Public Policy 21, Supplement: The Canadian Experience of the Lifetime Capital Gains Exemption* (October): S116–S135.

Joulfaian, David and David Richardson (2001). Who Takes Advantage of Tax-Deferred Saving Programs? Evidence from Federal Income Tax Data. *National Tax Journal* 54, 3 (September): 669–88.

Keuschnigg, Christian, and Soren Bo Nielsen (2004). Start-ups, Venture Capitalist, and the Capital Gains Tax. *Journal of Public Economics* 88: 1011–42.

King, Robert G., and Sergio Rebelo (1990). Public Policy and Economic Growth: Developing Neoclassical Implications. *Journal of Political Economy* 98, 5: 126–50.

Klevmarken, N. Anders (2000). Did the Tax Cuts Increase Hours of Work? A Statistical Analysis of a Natural Experiment. *Kyklos* 53: 337–62.

Kneller, Richard, Michael F. Bleaney and Norman Gemmell (1999). Fiscal Policy and Growth: Evidence from OECD Countries. *Journal of Public Economics* 74, 2: 171–90.

Koester, B. Reinhard, and Roger C. Kormendi (1989). Taxation, Aggregate Activity and Economic Growth: Cross-Country Evidence on Some Supply-Side Hypothesis. *Economic Inquiry* 27, 3 (July): 367–86.

Landsman, Wayne, and Douglas Shackelford (1995). The Lock-in Effect of Capital Gains Taxes: Evidence from the RJR Nabisco Leveraged Buyout. *National Tax Journal* 48, 2: 245–59.

Landsman, Wayne, Douglas Shackelford, and Robert Yetman (2002). The Determinants of Capital Gains Tax Compliance: Evidence from the RJR Nabisco Leveraged Buyout. *Journal of Public Economics* 84: 47–74.

Lee, Young, and Roger H. Gordon (2005). Tax Structure and Economic Growth. *Journal of Public Economics* 89: 1027–43.

Long, E. James (1988). Taxation and IRA Participation: Re-Examination and Conformation. *National Tax Journal* 41, 4 (December): 585–89.

McKenzie, Kenneth, and Aileen Thompson (1997). *Taxes, the Cost of Capital, and Investment: A Comparison of Canada and the United States*. Working paper 97-3, prepared for the Technical Committee on Business Taxation.

Milesi-Ferretti, Maria Gian, and Nouriel Roubini (1998). Growth Effects of Income and Consumption Taxes. *Journal of Money, Credit, and Banking* 30, 4: 721–44.

Milligan, Kevin (2002). Tax-preferred Savings Accounts and Marginal Tax Rates: Evidence on RRSP Participation. *Canadian Journal of Economics* 35, 3 (August): 436–56.

Milligan, Kevin, Jack Mintz, and Thomas A. Wilson (1999). *Capital Gains Taxation: Recent Empirical Evidence*. Working paper. The Heward Stikeman Institute.

Mullen, K. John, and Martin Williams (1994). Marginal Tax Rates and State Economic Growth. *Regional Science and Urban Economics* 24, 6 (December): 687–705.

O'Neil, Cherie J., and G. Rodney Thompson (1987). Participation in Individual Retirement Accounts: An Empirical Investigation. *National Tax Journal* 40, 4: 617–24.

Ohanian, Lee, Andrea Raffo, and Richard Rogerson (2006). *Long-term Changes in Labor Supply and Taxes: Evidence from OECD Countries, 1956–2004*. NBER working paper 12786. National Bureau of Economic Research.

Padovano, Fabio, and Emma Galli (2001). Tax Rates and Economic Growth in OECD Countries (1950–1990). *Economic Inquiry* 39, 1 (January): 44–57.

Padovano, Fabio, and Emma Galli (2002). Comparing the Growth Effects of Marginal vs. Average Tax Rates and Progressivity. *European Journal of Political Economy* 18: 529–44.

Poterba, James (1989). Venture Capital and Capital Gains Taxation. In Lawrence H. Summers, ed., *Tax Policy and the Economy* (MIT Press): 47–67.

Prescott, Edward C. (2004). Why Do Americans Work So Much More than Europeans? *Federal Reserve Bank of Minneapolis Quarterly Review* 28, 1 (July): 2–13.

Rebelo, Sergio. (1991). Long-Run Policy Analysis and Long-Run Growth. *Journal of Political Economy* 99, 3: 500–21.

Romer, Christina D., and David. H. Romer (2007). *The Macroeconomic Effects of Tax Changes: Estimates Based on a New Measure of Fiscal Shocks*. NBER working paper 13264. National Bureau of Economic Research.

Shackelford, Douglas (2000). Stock Market Reaction to Capital Gains Tax Changes: Empirical Evidence from the 1997 and 1998 Tax Acts. *Tax Policy and the Economy* 14: 67–92.

Schumpeter, Joseph A. (1942 / 1976). *Capitalism, Socialism, and Democracy.* Harper and Brothers / Harper Colophon.

Stuart, Charles E. (1981). Swedish Tax Rates, Labor Supply, and Tax Revenues. *Journal of Political Economy* 89, 5: 1020–38.

Sundstrom, Marianne (1991). Part-time Work in Sweden: Trends and Equality Effects. *Journal of Economic Issues* 25, 1: 167–78.

Thurston, K. Norman (2002). Physician Behavioral Responses to Variation in Marginal Income Tax Rates: Longitudinal Evidence. *Applied Economics* 34: 2093–104.

Thurston, Norman, and Anne M. Libby (2000). Taxes and Physicians' Use of Ancillary Health Labour. *Journal of Human Resources* 35, 2: 259–78.

Veldhuis, Niels, and Jason Clemens (2007). *Productivity, Prosperity, and Business Taxes.* Studies in Economic Prosperity 3. The Fraser Institute.

Veldhuis, Niels, Keith Godin, and Jason Clemens (2007). *The Economic Costs of Capital Gains Taxes.* Studies in Entrepreneurship and Markets 4. The Fraser Institute.

Ventura, Gustavo (1999). Flat Tax Reform: A Quantitative Exploration. *Journal of Economic Dynamics & Control* 23: 1425–58.

Widmalm, Frida (2001). Tax Structure and Growth: Are Some Taxes Better than Others? *Public Choice* 107: 199–219.

Ziliak, James, and Thomas Kniesner (2005). The Effects of Income Taxation on Consumption and Labor Supply. *Journal of Labour Economics* 23, 4: 769–96.

Ziliak, P. James, and Thomas J. Kniesner (1999). Estimating Life Cycle Labor Supply Tax Effects. *Journal of Political Economy* 107, 2 (April): 326–59.

Chapter 2

Not All Taxes Are Created Equal

Jason Clemens and Niels Veldhuis

Economic efficiency[1] is a key issue in tax policy that is frequently ignored in public policy debates on taxation. However, there is great reason to focus on efficiency because not all taxes are created equal: the economic costs of taxes differ and some taxes impose greater costs on society than others. Societies should rely more on the less costly taxes and less on the more costly taxes. There are, of course, other policy considerations in determining tax policy such as equity (often referred to as fairness) and simplicity[2] but in this chapter we focus on economic efficiency.

Section 1 reviews research on the cost of different taxes and provides compelling evidence that certain types of taxes impose much higher costs on society than others. Section 2 compares Canada's tax

---

1 ◆ This chapter relies heavily on a previously published study, *Tax Efficiency: Not All Taxes Are Created Equal* (Clemens, Veldhuis, and Palacios, 2007).

2 ◆ Equity or fairness refers to both horizontal equity (individuals and households with similar incomes should face similar tax burdens) and vertical equity (individuals and households pay more tax as their incomes increase). While not central to this study, these additional tests of equity and simplicity are critical since they, along with efficiency, influence what forms of taxation a jurisdiction uses. For example, if a jurisdiction is unconcerned with equity (fairness), then it can use lump-sum taxes, which impose no efficiency costs. For further information, see Emes et al., 2001; Clemens et al., 2003; Ott and Vegari, 2003; and Slemrod, 1994.

mix to those of the 29 other industrialized countries that form the Organisation for Economic Co-operation and Development (OECD). It provides data showing that Canada's tax mix is inefficient and uncompetitive in comparison to that of most other industrialized countries, which provides a rationale for changing our mix of taxes. Section 3 explains that a flat tax, since it is a consumption tax, would improve the efficiency of Canada's mix of taxes.

1 ◆ Costs of taxation

The costs to society of government taxation are not limited to the amount of the taxes imposed.[3] Individuals and businesses incur three additional costs. First, there are efficiency costs, which arise because taxes change people's behavior. They do so by changing the prices that households pay for the goods and services they consume and by changing the after-tax returns they receive from the inputs (land, labor, and capital) that they provide. Depending on the design of a specific tax, these changes can lead to such undesirable results as less savings, investment, work effort, risk-taking, and entrepreneurship than would otherwise be the case.

The second of the additional costs is referred to as compliance costs. These costs—to name but a few—include the time and expenses that individuals and businesses incur to maintain proper records, undertake tax planning, file necessary reports, and calculate necessary remittances. These costs are all associated with conforming to tax regulations.

The third additional cost that society bears is the administrative cost of taxation. These costs are incurred by governments in order to collect and enforce taxes but are ultimately paid by members of the society. Taxpayers have to pay yet higher taxes to pay for the cost of government. These administrative costs along with compliance costs are discussed at length in chapter 3 of this book. The sum of these costs (tax liability, efficiency costs, compliance expenses, and government administrative costs) comprises the total cost of government taxation.

---

3 ◆ For an overview of the costs associated with taxation, see US GAO, 2005.

Efficiency cost of taxes

Taxes impose efficiency costs on society because they change the way individuals, families, and businesses behave. Individuals and firms make decisions based on prices. Raise the price of a good and consumers will likely purchase it less, and substitute alternatives (i.e. other goods) in its place. Similarly, raise the price of a business input and the business will search for ways to compensate for the increased costs through substitution and innovation. Taxes change the relative prices of goods, services, and inputs by making some inputs more expensive and others relatively less so. This change in prices distorts a firm's production decisions— what to produce, and how, where, and when to produce it. Taxes can also reduce the net return that workers get from working, or taking advanced training or education, and the net returns that investors get from employing their capital in one industry rather than another.

For example, an increase in an employer's payroll tax means that labor, at least in the short term,[4] has become more expensive. When faced with higher labor costs, firms, particularly labor-intensive ones, will look for ways to mitigate the increased expense by substituting capital, such as machinery and equipment, for labor.

Taxes on savings, such as personal income taxes on interest, dividends, and capital gains, and taxes on capital such as corporate income taxes and capital taxes, reduce investors' rates of return (after-tax) and so reduce the incentive to save and invest.[5] This can have a profound effect on productivity-enhancing investment, and ultimately on workers' wage rates. Indeed, in its recent report, *Advantage Canada*, the federal government explained the importance of business investment:

> Business investment is critical to our long-term prosperity. It yields innovation and growth, with more jobs and higher wages for

---

4 ◆ Over the longer term, payroll taxes become part of the overall cost of labor in terms of compensation. In other words, payroll taxes are borne by workers through lower wage rates.

5 ◆ For more information on Canada's unique corporate capital taxes, see Clemens et al., 2002; for information on the ultimate incidence of business taxes, see Clemens and Veldhuis, 2003.

Canadian workers. High investment taxes are harmful because they reduce the returns from investment, thereby reducing the amount of investment that takes place in Canada. (Canada, Department of Finance, 2006b: 73)

Another example of taxes affecting behavior is personal income tax, which affects the supply of labor by decreasing after-tax wages. For instance, the drop in after-tax wages caused by personal income taxes affects how much people work (the total number of hours worked) and their overall work effort.[6] The federal government report that outlined problems with Canada's taxes on savings and investment also identified serious problems with Canada's personal income taxes. For example, *Advantage Canada* notes that "Canada's tax burden on highly skilled workers is too high relative to other countries," and that the country needs to lower these marginal rates in order to "attract and retain highly skilled workers; encourage more Canadians to realize their full potential and improve the standard of living in Canada; encourage all workers to invest in training and education" (Canada, Department of Finance, 2006b: 46).

Finally, sales taxes also affect the incentive to work because they reduce a worker's real wage rate by increasing the prices of consumer goods.[7] In addition, sales taxes that are levied on the inputs purchased by firms (a common feature of the provincial retail sales taxes)[8] drive up businesses' costs and reduce their competitiveness.[9]

---

6 ◆ For further information on these incentive effects and their influence, see Clemens et al., 2004; and Veldhuis and Clemens, 2006.

7 ◆ Note that sales taxes do not distort intertemporal consumption decisions if the tax rate is constant.

8 ◆ British Columbia, Saskatchewan, Manitoba, Ontario, and Prince Edward Island all apply their provincial sales taxes to business inputs and capital goods, albeit to varying degrees due to the presence of exemptions on certain types of goods.

9 ◆ The federal government estimates that harmonization of provincial retail sales taxes with the GST, which would exempt business inputs and capital goods, would materially reduce the cost of new investment. For example, *Advantage Canada* indicates that such harmonization in Ontario would reduce the marginal effective

Research on marginal efficiency cost

Numerous academic and government-commissioned studies have estimated the economic costs of different types of taxes. A critical contribution to this field was made in the early 1970s by Nobel Laureate James Mirrlees, who developed the theory of optimal taxation. The core of Mirrlees' work was that governments should achieve given revenue requirements by choosing taxes that have the best social welfare outcome (Mirrlees, 1971 and 1972; Diamond and Mirrlees, 1971).

The research summarized in the next few paragraphs, which survey a number of key studies on the efficiency costs of taxes for Canada and the United States, relies on what is referred to as marginal efficiency cost (MEC)[10] or marginal excess burden (MEB) calculations. The MEC methodology provides a mechanism by which to estimate the cost of different taxes. Specifically, the MEC calculates the efficiency cost of raising one additional dollar of revenue.[11]

---

tax rate by 9 percentage points (Canada, Department of Finance, 2006b: 76). Note that the large gains from harmonization are restricted to those provinces that apply non-integrated provincial sales taxes: British Columbia, Saskatchewan, Manitoba, Ontario, and Prine Edward Island. In its 2006 *Economic Survey of Canada*, the OECD concludes that harmonization of provincial sales taxes with the GST would "provide a more productivity-friendly environment" (OECD, 2006a: 12).

10 ◆ The marginal efficiency cost (MEC) of taxes should not be confused with another important concept, the marginal cost of public funds (MCPF). The MCPF is the ratio of the economic costs of taxation to the value of the tax revenues raised to finance a government project. For instance, an MCPF of $1.50 indicates that an additional dollar of tax revenue imposes a cost of $1.50 on the economy. In this framework, government spending can only be justified if it produces more than a $1.50 worth of benefits. For further discussion of MCPF, see Browning, 1976, 1987; and Dahlby, 1998.

11 ◆ Note that the marginal efficiency cost of taxes are estimates of the cost of raising one additional dollar of revenue. They are, therefore, measures of marginal or incremental cost and should be used to measure the benefits of small or incremental tax shifts. The MEC cannot be used to measure the total, or even the average, cost of taxes. In other words, MECs should be used cautiously, if at all, when estimating large-scale tax shifts when the relationship between the tax rate and efficiency cost is non-linear.

The MEC in Canada

The federal Department of Finance has calculated, and the Organisation for Economic Co-operation and Development (OECD) has published, the MEC estimates for Canadian taxes (OECD, 1997). As will be evident throughout this summary, capital-based taxes tend to impose much higher costs on society due to their incentive effects (lower savings, less investment, and ultimately slower income growth based on lower productivity) than other taxes deemed to be less costly (more efficient) such as consumption taxes. Table 2.1 summarizs the results from the study. The Department of Finance concluded that corporate income taxes impose a marginal cost of $1.55 (MEC) for one additional dollar of revenue.[12] This compares with a cost of $0.17 for an additional dollar of revenue raised through consumption taxes.[13] Payroll taxes were also determined to impose relatively low costs on society.

More recently, the federal department of finance published a study by Baylor and Beauséjour (2004) that calculated the long-term economic costs imposed by the main taxes used in Canada.[14] Figure 2.1 shows the results of the study. The results of Baylor and Beauséjour (2004) support the earlier MEC estimate. Capital-based taxes, such as sales taxes on capital goods purchased by businesses, personal income taxes

---

12 ◆ The Department of Finance (OECD, 1997) found much higher costs for a general corporate income tax than the later study by Baylor and Beauséjour (2004).

13 ◆ There are critical differences between the federal goods and services tax (GST) and the provincial sales taxes (often referred to as retail sales taxes) in many provinces. Specifically, provinces with independent sales taxes (British Columbia, Saskatchewan, Manitoba, Ontario, and Prince Edward Island) apply them to business inputs such as machinery and equipment. The federal GST, and sales taxes in provinces that have harmonized their retail sales taxes with the GST, exempt such business inputs, ensuring that the tax actually applies to final consumption. Quebec's provincial sales tax, while not harmonized with the GST, is a value-added tax that does not apply to business inputs and capital goods. This is critical since the application of a sales tax to business inputs effectively taxes capital, not consumption.

14 ◆ The study calculated the benefits from reducing taxes and assumed that the tax revenues lost due to the tax cuts were offset by a non-distortionary lump-sum tax increase. In other words, the tax changes were revenue neutral. In addition, lump-sum taxes are assumed not to distort individual and firm behavior because they do not alter relative prices. See Mankiw (2004), for further details on lump-sum taxes.

Table 2.1: Estimates of marginal efficiency costs (MEC) for selected Canadian taxes

	MEC (CDN$)
Corporate income tax	$1.55
Personal income tax	$0.56
Payroll tax	$0.27
Sales tax	$0.17

Source: OECD, 1997.

Figure 2.1: Welfare gains from tax reductions[1]

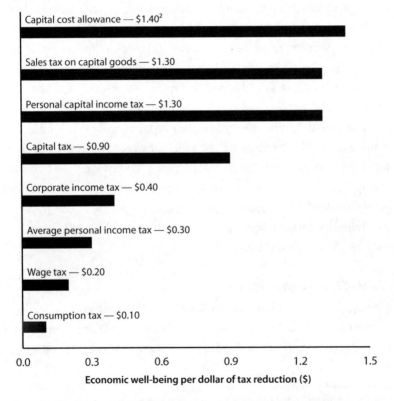

Capital cost allowance — $1.40[2]

Sales tax on capital goods — $1.30

Personal capital income tax — $1.30

Capital tax — $0.90

Corporate income tax — $0.40

Average personal income tax — $0.30

Wage tax — $0.20

Consumption tax — $0.10

Economic well-being per dollar of tax reduction ($)

Note 1: Revenue loss is assumed to be recovered through "lump-sum" taxation. Welfare gains are calculated as the gain in economic well-being per dollar of tax reduction.

Note 2: The estimate for an increase in capital cost allowances (CCA) is for new capital only. Increasing CCA is not a tax reduction per se but rather an increase in a deduction against corporate income taxes.

Source: Baylor and Beauséjour, 2004.

on investment income, capital taxes imposed on large firms, and corporate income taxes, impose substantially larger burdens on society than payroll and goods and services (consumption) taxes. For example, decreasing personal income taxes on capital (dividends, capital gains, and interest income) by $1 and imposing an off-setting $1 increase in sales taxes would result in a net increase ($1.30 – $0.10) of $1.20 in society's well-being (figure 2.1).

Along similar lines, Quebec's ministry of finance recently calculated the benefits to Quebec's economy from reducing different provincial taxes (Québec, Ministère des Finances, 2006). The results of the analysis, which are summarized in table 2.2, corroborate Baylor and Beauséjour's findings: Quebec's department of finance found that capital-based and income taxes impose significantly higher costs on society than sales taxes. The ministry estimated that reducing taxes on capital by $1 would result in an increase in inflation-adjusted gross domestic product (GDP) of $1.21, whereas a $1 reduction in Quebec's sales tax (QST) would increase inflation-adjusted (real) GDP by $0.54 (table 2.2).[15]

Although there are differences in the types of economic models and frameworks used to measure the efficiency costs of imposing taxes, leading to different estimates of MECs for specific taxes, the two studies by Canada's Department of Finance as well as the study by the government of Quebec all concluded that capital-based taxes imposed much higher costs on society compared to other, more efficient, taxes such as consumption taxes.

The MEC in the United States

Among the most widely cited calculations of estimated marginal efficiency costs (MEC) are those by Harvard Professor, Dale Jorgensen and his colleague, Kun-Young Yun (1991).[16] Jorgensen and Yun's estimates

---

15 ◆ The Ministry assumed that the tax revenues lost due to the tax cuts were offset by a fixed (non-distortionary) tax.

16 ◆ There are important studies of MEC for other countries, although the bulk of such work has examined the United States. For example, Professors Erwin Diewert and Denis Lawrence (1996) estimated the MEC of selected taxes for New Zealand between 1971 to 1991.

Table 2.2: Impact on real GDP per dollar of tax reduction in Quebec[1]

Tax on Capital	$1.21
Personal Income Tax	$0.74
Payroll Tax	$0.66
Quebec Sales Tax (QST)	$0.54
Total[2]	$0.74

Note 1: Estimates are revenue neutral. The loss in revenue is offset by a fixed tax.

Note 2: The total corresponds to a proportional reduction in all taxes.

Source: Québec, Ministère des Finances, 2006: 11.

of the MEC of select US taxes indicate significant variation in the economic costs of different taxes and support the findings from the three Canadian studies cited above (table 2.3). Specifically, capital-based taxes (MEC = $0.92) and corporate income taxes (MEC = $0.84) were shown to impose much higher costs than other, more efficient types of tax such as the sales tax (MEC = $0.26). In other words, it costs the economy $0.26 to raise an additional dollar of revenue using consumption taxes, but $0.92 to raise an additional dollar of tax revenue using capital-based income taxes.

Another important study that calculated the costs of different taxes was completed by Ballard, Shoven, and Whalley in 1985 and published in the prestigious *American Economic Review*. The study reported MEC

Table 2.3: Estimates of Marginal Efficiency Costs (MEC) for Select US Taxes

	MEC ($CDN)
Capital income taxes (individual & corporate)	$0.92
Corporate income tax	$0.84
Individual income tax	$0.60
Payroll tax	$0.48
Sales tax	$0.26

Source: Jorgenson and Yun, 1991.

Table 2.4: **Marginal excess burden from raising extra revenue from specific portions of the tax system**

All taxes	$0.170
Capital taxes at industry level	$0.181
Income taxes	$0.163
Labour taxes at industry level	$0.121
Sales taxes on commodities	$0.035

Note: The original table provided four cost estimates. We have presented only what we deemed to be the most "conservative" cost estimate. This table is, therefore, only a partial presentation of the table found in Ballard et al., 1985.

Source: Ballard et al., 1985: 136.

estimates for a broad range of taxes in the United States (table 2.4). The authors calculated that each dollar of additional tax revenue imposed costs in the range of $0.17 to $0.56 on the American economy. As observed in the previous studies, however, there were across-the-board differences in the costs for different taxes. The authors found that the efficiency costs of sales taxes (which were defined to exclude taxes on alcohol, tobacco, and gasoline)[17] were significantly lower ($0.035) compared to other taxes, such as capital taxes ($0.181), income taxes ($0.163), and payroll taxes ($0.121).

Conclusion

Estimates of the marginal efficiency costs of both American and Canadian taxes indicate that sales (consumption) and payroll (wage and salary) taxes are much less costly (more efficient) than taxes on capital or the return to capital. As a result, there are economic gains available to taxpayers in both Canada and elsewhere from shifting the tax mix away from capital-based taxes to more efficient taxes such as those based on consumption.

---

17 ◆ For a discussion of consumption taxes on cigarettes and alcohol, see Hines, 2006.

2 ◆ The tax mix in Canada and the rest of the OECD

The costs imposed on an economy by different tax mixes can have competitive implications. A jurisdiction that chooses a more efficient mix of taxes can out-perform its competitors. This section examines the kinds of taxes upon which Canadian governments (federal, provincial, and local) rely and compares Canada's tax mix to those of the 29 other industrialized countries of the Organisation for Economic Co-operation and Development (OECD). Note that the comparisons are not based on tax rates but rather the composition of total tax revenues.

The tax mix in 2004

Table 2.5 shows the tax mix across six major categories of government revenue[18] for the 30 OECD countries as well as an OECD average for 2004, the most recent year for which comparable data are available. The analysis examines the composition of total tax revenues for OECD countries across the following categories: (1) income and profit taxes, (2) social security taxes,[19] (3) payroll taxes, (4) property taxes, (5) goods and services taxes (consumption), and (6) other taxes.

Canada has the fourth highest reliance on income and profit taxes among OECD countries. At 46.5% of total tax revenues, income and profit taxes constitute nearly half of all tax revenues for governments in Canada (table 2.5). Canada's use of income and profit taxes is 35.2% higher than the OECD average of 34.4%. This is particularly important given the research presented in the first section showing that taxes on profit and investment tend to impose higher economic costs than other, more efficient, types of taxes. On the other hand, sales tax, which is one of the most efficient types of tax, represents a much lower percentage of total tax revenues in Canada than in other industrialized countries. Specifically, Canada ranks 24th out of 30 OECD countries in terms of

---

18 ◆ For a definition of the six categories, see "Annex A: The OECD Classification of Taxes and Interpretative Guide" in OECD, 2006b: 281.

19 ◆ In many countries, social security taxes are payroll or wage taxes. For further details, see "Annex A," OECD, 2006b.

Table 2.5: Tax revenue from six major categories of government revenue as percentage of total taxation, 2004

	Income & profits	Social security	Payroll	Property	Goods & services	Other
Australia	58.4	—	4.4	8.7	28.5	—
Austria	29.4	33.9	6.1	1.3	28.2	0.9
Belgium	38.6	31.3	—	3.9	25.0	0.0
Canada	46.5	15.2	2.0	10.2	25.9	0.3
Czech Republic	25.1	42.3	—	1.1	31.2	0.0
Denmark[1]	60.3	2.4	0.4	3.8	32.7	0.0
Finland	38.6	26.8	—	2.6	31.7	0.1
France[1]	23.3	37.1	2.6	7.6	25.6	3.6
Germany	27.3	40.7	—	2.5	29.2	0.0
Greece	23.5	34.7	—	4.4	37.1	—
Hungary	23.6	30.1	2.3	2.3	40.8	0.8
Iceland	44.0	8.3	—	6.3	41.1	0.2
Ireland	39.3	15.0	0.6	6.9	37.8	—
Italy	31.4	30.3	—	6.1	26.4	5.5
Japan	32.0	37.7	—	10.0	20.0	0.3
Korea	27.9	20.7	0.2	11.3	36.3	3.5
Luxembourg	33.2	28.3	—	7.8	30.4	0.2
Mexico	24.6	16.5	1.2	1.6	55.5	0.6
Netherlands	24.6	36.9	—	5.3	32.0	0.4
New Zealand	61.1	—	—	5.0	33.8	—
Norway[1]	46.2	21.6	—	2.6	29.7	—
Poland	17.9	40.9	0.7	3.8	36.0	—
Portugal	24.2	31.8	—	4.6	38.6	0.5
Slovak Republic[1]	18.8	39.4	—	1.8	39.8	—
Spain[1]	28.2	34.8	—	8.1	28.0	0.4
Sweden	37.7	28.4	4.7	3.1	25.8	0.1
Switzerland	43.4	24.4	—	8.5	23.7	—
Turkey	22.1	23.9	—	3.1	47.7	3.2
United Kingdom	36.8	18.8	—	12.0	32.0	—
United States	43.4	26.3	—	12.0	18.3	—
Unweighted average:						
OECD Total	34.4	25.9	0.9	5.6	32.3	0.7

Note 1: The total tax revenues have been reduced by the amount of capital transfer. The capital transfer has been allocated among tax categories in proportion to the reported tax revenue.

Source: Organisation for Economic Co-operation and Development, 2006b: 73, table 7.

its reliance on taxes on goods and services. Only 25.9% of total tax revenues in Canada are collected from such taxes (table 2.5).[20] This compares unfavorably with an OECD average of 32.3%. Canada also ranks low (25th of 30 OECD countries) in its use of social-security taxes. In Canada, social security taxes make up 15.2% of total tax revenues compared to an OECD average of 25.9% (table 2.5).[21]

Finally, Canada ranks fourth in its use of property taxes, with 10.2% of its total tax revenue coming from such taxes (table 2.5).[22] This is nearly the double the OECD average of 5.6%. Note that part of the property-tax base is capital invested by businesses in structures (plants) as well as investments in housing by households.

An analysis of the composition of Canada's tax mix in table 2.5 indicates that this country relies too heavily on high-cost taxes such as those on investment income and profit and too little on less distortion- ary taxes such as those on goods and services. There is some room for ambiguity here because our personal income-tax system has elements of consumption taxation in it, given the tax treatment of RRSPs, pen- sions, and the non-taxation of the return on owner-occupied housing. To the extent that our tax system relies too much on high-cost sources of tax revenue, the Canadian economy grows at a lower rate than might be possible with a more efficient tax system.

---

20 ◆ An important aspect of this comparison is not readily observable: many per- sonal income-tax systems behave as consumption taxes. In Canada, for example, the personal income-tax system is actually a hybrid tax, combining features of con- sumption and pure income taxes, because it allows for savings to be sheltered in the form of registered savings plans, such as RRSPs and pensions. In other words, for many taxpayers in Canada, the personal income-tax system does not tax sav- ings. Readers should be cautious, therefore, in drawing any definitive conclusions about the extent of income taxes compared to consumption taxes in the OECD countries. See Poddar and English, 1999 for additional information on Canada's mixed income-tax system.

21 ◆ This result is somewhat mitigated by the use of payroll taxes in some Canadian provinces. Only 11 of the 30 OECD countries use what would be considered a pay- roll tax under the OECD definitions of tax revenue. Payroll taxes would behave as social-security taxes and thus impose similar costs on the economy.

22 ◆ The data include property taxes derived both from residential and business sources.

Trends in the compostition of Canada's tax mix, 1965–2004

Table 2.6 contains summary data for Canada and the OECD average for five of the six major categories of tax revenue covered by
the OECD (2006b) for the period from 1965 to 2004.[23] During this
period, Canada's taxes on personal income have become an increasing
percentage of total tax revenues: the country's reliance on personal
income taxes has increased from 22.6% of the total tax take in 1965
to 35.1% in 2004. However, this level (35.1%) is down from its peak
in 1990 when personal income taxes reached 40.8% of total tax revenues. This trend of increasingly relying on personal income taxes
contrasts starkly with the overall OECD average, which saw a slight
decline in such taxes: 26.2% of total taxes in 1965 versus 24.6% in 2004.
Canada's reliance on corporate income as a source of tax revenue actually declined between 1965 and 2004. As a share of total tax revenues,
corporate income tax dropped from 14.9% in 1965 to 10.3% in 2004
(table 2.6). Meanwhile, the OECD average increased slightly from 8.8%
in 1965 to 9.6% in 2004.

The dramatic increase in Canada's reliance on personal income
taxes is matched by a nearly equal decline in its reliance on taxes on
goods and services (consumption). The proportion of taxes raised
from goods and services declined from 40.5% in 1965 to 25.9% in 2004
(table 2.6). While the OECD average for taxes on goods and services as
a share of total tax revenue also declined over the same period, from
38.2% to 32.3%, the decline was much smaller than in Canada.

Interestingly, the most dramatic change is in social-security contributions. In Canada, this tax category increased from 5.6% of total
tax revenue in 1965 to 15.2% in 2004, a 171.4% increase (table 2.6). The
increase for the OECD average was notable, but less stark: from 17.7%
in 1965 to 25.9% in 2004—a 46.3% increase.

In both Canada and the OECD generally, the use of property taxes
has been declining. Canada's reliance on property taxes has declined
from 14.3% of total tax revenues in 1965 to 10.2% in 2004 (table 2.6).

---

23 ◆ The discussion is restricted to five tax categories because the use of payroll
taxes is quite limited. Canada's reliance on such taxes amounts to only 2.0% of
total tax revenue for 2004 and the OECD average is a mere 0.8%.

Table 2.6: Comparative tax revenues for Canada and the OECD, 1965–2004

	1965	1970	1975	1980	1985	1990	1995	2000	2003	2004
1 Taxes on personal income as percentage of total taxation										
Canada	22.6	32.4	32.8	34.1	35.2	40.8	37.5	36.8	34.8	35.1
OECD average	26.2	27.9	29.8	31.3	29.7	29.7	27.1	26.0	25.0	24.6
2 Taxes on corporate income as percentage of total taxation.										
Canada	14.9	11.3	13.6	11.6	8.2	7.0	8.2	12.2	9.5	10.3
OECD average	8.8	8.8	7.6	7.6	8.0	8.0	8.1	10.1	9.3	9.6
3 Taxes on goods and services as percentage of total taxation										
Canada	40.5	31.7	32.0	32.6	31.8	25.8	25.4	24.2	26.3	25.9
OECD average	38.2	36.0	32.7	32.4	33.7	31.9	32.4	31.6	32.1	32.3
4 Social security contributions as percentage of total taxation										
Canada	5.6	9.7	10.0	10.5	13.5	12.1	14.0	13.6	15.7	15.2
OECD average	17.7	19.1	22	22.1	22.2	22.3	24.7	24.5	26.1	25.9
5 Taxes on payroll and workforce as percentage of total taxation										
Canada	-	-	-	-	-	2.3	2.2	2.1	2.1	2.0
OECD average	1.0	1.1	1.3	1.3	1.1	1.0	0.9	0.9	0.9	0.8
6 Taxes on property as a percentage of total taxation										
Canada	14.3	12.8	9.5	9.1	9.3	10.0	10.7	9.5	10.2	10.2
OECD average	7.9	7.1	6.3	5.3	5.2	5.7	5.5	5.5	5.6	5.6

Source: Organisation for Economic Co-operation and Development, 2006b: tables 11, 13, 15, 21, 23, and 25.

Similarly, the average use of property taxes in the OECD has decreased from 7.9% of total tax revenues to 5.6% over the same period. An important note, however, is that Canada still uses nearly double the level of property taxes as a share of total tax revenue as the OECD average.

3 ◆ **Flat tax as a consumption tax**

It should be abundantly clear that different taxes impose different costs. Among these taxes, consumption taxes impose the lowest costs while capital-based taxes tend to impose the highest costs. In addition, Canada is unique within the industrialized world (OECD) in terms of our comparatively high reliance on income and profit taxes and our relatively low reliance on consumption taxes. Canada tends to rely more than our competitors on costly taxes while relying less on lower cost taxes.

What is often misunderstood about the flat tax is that it more than likely behaves as a consumption tax.[24] The flat-tax proposal for Canada discussed elsewhere in this volume as well as the many flat-tax systems around the world summarized in chapter 4 operate as a consumption tax to the extent they exempt savings. Recall that consumption taxes are by design taxes imposed on consumption. Consumption is simply that portion of income that is spent rather than saved. Thus, income-tax systems that exempt savings, either in part or in whole, act as a consumption tax. The real difference is simply where and when the tax is applied. Most consumption taxes come in the form of sales taxes, which are assessed at the point of purchase. A person who buys a good or service pays the sales tax at the time and place of the purchase. Income taxes, on the other hand, will exempt savings on a periodic basis based on tax reporting. That is, taxpayers will file their income taxes and receive exemptions from tax for their savings. The end result of both approaches, however, is to exempt savings from taxation, which results in only consumption being taxed.

Canada has an opportunity to implement a flat-tax system as outlined elsewhere in this volume while at the same time relying to a much greater degree on a consumption-tax system, which imposes much lower economic costs on society. This would make our tax system much more competitive with other industrialized countries.

---

24 ◆ Indeed, Canada's current income-tax system already behaves to a certain extent as a consumption tax for a majority of taxpayers. See Poddar and English, 1999.

References

Ballard, Charles L., John B. Shoven, and John Whalley (1985). General Equilibrium Computations of the Marginal Welfare Costs of Taxes in the United States. *American Economic Review* 75, 1: 128–38.

Bator, Francis (1957). The Simple Analytics of Welfare Maximization. *American Economic Review* 47, 1: 22–44.

Baumol, William J. (1972). On Taxation and the Control of Externalities. *American Economic Review* 62, 3: 307–22.

Baylor, Maximilian, and Louise Beauséjour (2004). *Taxation and Economic Efficiency: Results from a Canadian CGE Model.* Working paper 2004-10 (November). Canada, Department of Finance.

Boadway, Robin, and Michael Keen (2000). *Redistribution: Handbook of Income Distribution.* Volume 1. Elsevier Science, North-Holland.

Browning, Edgar K. (1976). The Marginal Cost of Public Funds. *Journal of Political Economy* 84, 2: 283–98.

Browning, Edgar K. (1987). On the Marginal Welfare Cost of Taxation. *American Economic Review* 77, 1: 11–23.

Canada, Department of Finance (2005). *Tax Expenditures and Evaluations.* Government of Canada.

Canada, Department of Finance (2006a). *Economic and Fiscal Update 2006.* Government of Canada.

Canada, Department of Finance (2006b). *Advantage Canada: Building a Strong Economy for Canadians.* Government of Canada.

Canada, Department of Finance (2006). *Tax Expenditures and Evaluations*. Government of Canada.

Chen, Duanjie (2000). *The Marginal Effective Tax Rate: The Only Tax Rate that Matters in Capital Allocation*. Backgrounder (August 22). CD Howe Institute.

Chen, Duanjie, and Jack Mintz (2006). *Federal/Provincial Combined Marginal Effective Tax Rates on Capital 1997–2006, 2010*. CD Howe Institute.

Clemens, Jason, and Niels Veldhuis (2003). Who Pays Business Taxes? A Different View. Fraser Forum (October): 30-31.

Clemens, Jason, Niels Veldhuis, and Milagros Palacios (2007). *Tax Efficiency: Not All Taxes Are Created Equal*. The Fraser Institute.

Clemens, Jason, Joel Emes, and Rodger Scott (2002). *The Corporate Capital Tax: Canada's Most Damaging Tax*. Public Policy Sources 56. The Fraser Institute.

Clemens, Jason, Joel Emes, and Rodger Scott (2003). The Flat Tax—A Model for Reform of Personal and Business Taxes. In Herbert G. Grubel, ed., *Tax Reform in Canada: Our Path to Greater Prosperity* (The Fraser Institute): 53–76.

Clemens, Jason, N. Veldhuis, A. Karabegovic, and K. Godin (2004). Do Tax Rates Matter? *Fraser Forum* (July): 13–16.

Clemens, Jason, N. Veldhuis, and M. Palacios (2006). *Fiscal Balance, the GST, and Decentralization: An Opportunity for Reform*. Fraser Institute Digital Publication (October). The Fraser Institute. <http://www.fraserinstitute.ca/admin/books/files/FiscalBalanceGST.pdf>.

Dahlby, Beverly (1998). Progressive Taxation and the Social Marginal Cost of Public Funds. *Journal of Public Economics* 67, 1: 105–22.

Diamond, Peter, and James Mirrlees. (1971). Optimal Taxation and Public Production. *American Economic Review* 61, 1: 8–27; 261–78.

Diewert, W. Erwin, and Denis A. Lawrence (1996). The Deadweight Costs of Taxation in New Zealand. *Canadian Journal of Economics* 29, Special Issue, Part 2 (April): S658–S673.

Emes, Joel, and Jason Clemens (2001). *Flat Tax: Principles and Issues*. Critical Issues Bulletin. The Fraser Institute.

Erard, Brian (1997a). The Income Tax Compliance Burden on Canadian Big Business. Working Paper 97-2. Technical Committee on Business Taxation (April).

Erard, Brian (1997b). The Income Tax Compliance Burden on Small and Medium-sized Canadian Business. Working Paper 97-12. Technical Committee on Business Taxation (October).

Harris, Mike, and Preston Manning (2006). *Building Prosperity in a Canada Strong and Free*. A Canada Strong and Free/Pour un Canada fort et prospere, vol. IV. The Fraser Institute and the Montreal Economic Institute.

Hines, James R. Jr. (2006). Taxing Consumption and Other Sins. NBER paper 12730. National Bureau of Economic Research.

Jorgensen, Dale W., and Kun-Young Yun (1991). The Excess Burden of Taxation in the United States. *Journal of Accounting and Finance* 6, 4: 487–508.

Kesselman, Jonathan R. (2004). *Tax Design for a Northern Tiger*. Choices: Economic Policy and Growth 10, 1 (March). Institute for Research on Public Policy.

Mankiw, N. Gregory (2004). *Principles of Microeconomics*. 3rd ed. Thomson/South-Western.

Mankiw, Gregory, and Matthew Weinzierl (2006). Dynamic Scoring: A Back of the Envelope Guide. *Journal of Public Economics* 90, 8–9: 1415–33.

Mirrlees, James (1971). An exploration into the Theory of Optimal Income Taxation. *Review of Economic Studies* 38, 2: 175–208.

Mirrlees, James (1972). The Optimum Town. *Swedish Journal of Economics* 74, 1: 114–35.

Organisation for Economic Co-operation and Development (1997). *OECD Economic Survey: Canada*. OECD.

Organisation for Economic Co-operation and Development (2006a). *Economic Survey of Canada*. OECD

Organisation for Economic Co-operation and Development (2006b). *Revenue Statistics, 1965–2005*. OECD

Ott, Attiat F., and Sheila B. Vegari (2003). Tax Reform: Chasing the Elusive Dream. *Atlantic Economic Journal* 31, 3 (September): 266–82.

Poddar, Satyar, and Morley English (1999). Canadian Taxation of Personal Investment Income. *Canadian Tax Journal* 47, 5: 1270–304.

Québec, Ministère des Finances (2006). *2005-06 Budget: Budget Plan*. Gouvernement du Québec.

Salanie, Bernard (2003). *The Economics of Taxation*. MIT Press.

Stuart, Charles (1984). Welfare Costs per Dollar of Additional Tax Revenue in the United States. *American Economic Review* 74, 3: 352–62.

United States of America, General Accountability Office (2005). *Tax Policy: Summary of Estimates of the Costs of the Federal Tax System*. GAO-05-878. Government of the United States of America.

Veldhuis, Niels (2006). Presentation to the British Columbia Provincial Sales Tax Review Panel (January 19, 2006). The Fraser Institute. Unpublished paper available upon request.

Veldhuis, Niels, and Jason Clemens (2006). *Productivity, Prosperity, and Business Taxes*. Studies in Economic Prosperity 3. The Fraser Institute.

Chapter 3

Compliance and Administrative Costs of Taxation in Canada

François Vaillancourt & Jason Clemens

Taxes levied by government to finance public services reduce the resources available to members of society both directly and indirectly. The direct cost is simply the tax itself while the indirect costs include distortions in behavior[1] (the excess burden of taxation) and the resources consumed in the operation of the tax system. The goal of tax policy should be to raise a sufficient amount of resources for the government to provide services demanded by citizens in the least costly manner possible. That is, governments should minimize the amount of economic distortion caused by the imposition of taxes and be sensitive to the costs imposed on individuals and business when complying with tax laws and regulations (compliance costs) and the costs of managing and maintaining the tax system (administrative costs).

This chapter examines both compliance and administrative costs, which are far too often neglected in tax policy discussions. More specifically, this paper calculates an up-to-date estimate of total compliance and administrative costs for Canada and compares them with

---

1 ❖ For a review of evidence on behavioral costs of taxation, see Clemens, Veldhuis, & Palacios, 2007.

those reported in international research.[2] In some countries, recent studies have moved beyond measurement of compliance costs to focus on how the burden can be reduced, adopting a qualitative rather than quantitative approach. In the case of Canada, the lack of recent work on this issue requires us to focus on total costs.

Unfortunately, relatively little research has been undertaken in this area either in Canada or internationally, with Australia a notable exception. Canada has no consistent time series on compliance and administrative costs, and comparable figures across countries are similarly lacking.[3] The costs of a tax system, which include the indirect costs, are a key component of taxation and require greater and more consistent research.

The first section of this chapter outlines the various costs presented above and reviews the international research. The second section provides an estimate of these costs for Canada. Finally, there are conclusions, a brief set of recommendations, and two appendices listing studies of the compliance costs for individuals (1985–2006) and studies of the compliance costs for businesses (1985–2006).

1 ◆ **Compliance and administrative costs**

This section provides a brief definition of compliance and administrative costs. It also provides an overview of the international evidence on these costs.

Compliance costs

Compliance costs are those expenses incurred by individuals, families, and businesses to comply with tax regulations. These include the time and expenses incurred by individuals and businesses to maintain proper records, undertake tax planning, file necessary reports, and

---

2 ◆ The international estimates provided can only be used as rough comparisons since there are often large differences in the design and nature of tax systems in different countries. See Sandford, 1995 for further details on this point.

3 ◆ Cordova-Novion and Young, 2001 is an exception.

calculate required remittances.[4] They include both the costs incurred by individuals and businesses as well as fees paid to tax professionals such as accountants and lawyers. Costs incurred by businesses include collecting, managing, and remitting taxes paid by employees (Employment Insurance, Canada Pension Plan, etc.) to the government, the costs of paying the businesses own taxes, and in providing tax-related information to governments (statement of earned financial income, transactions and so on).

Administrative costs

Administrative costs are those incurred by governments to collect taxes and enforce tax regulations. These costs include collecting, administering, and managing the tax-collection system. They include the direct costs of the Canada Revenue Agency (CRA), which is responsible for administering and managing the Canadian tax system and related overhead. They also include indirect costs incurred by judicial and quasi-judicial bodies responsible for settling disputes between taxpayers and the government.

Review of Canadian and international research

This section provides an overview of the research completed to date on tax compliance costs both in Canada and abroad. It is designed to provide readers with some context for comparative purposes when studying the compliance cost calculations for Canada provided later in the paper. This overview of the research is organized into two parts: individuals and businesses. The first part summarizes the small amount of research on compliance costs for individuals. The second part focuses on compliance costs for businesses. The discussion differentiates between Canadian research and work completed internationally. The research presented is limited to taxes that are similar to those imposed

---

4 ◆ The research on compliance costs also sometimes refers to psychological costs. These costs relate to that fact that the time spent complying with tax regulations is generally an unpleasant experience and thus imposes costs on taxpayers. These costs have never been measured.

in Canada. The principal result of reviewing this research is that compliance costs tend to be significant, regressive with respect to the size of business, and increasing with the complexity of the tax environment.

While tax compliance costs are acknowledged as an important aspect of tax policy, there is still not as large or robust a body of scholarly work as is required to improve tax policy. For example, there are a limited number of comprehensive studies of the compliance costs for all taxes using a standardized methodology.[5] The standard practice of research in this field has been to calculate compliance costs for one or a few taxes in a specific region or country. This section summarizes the available research.[6]

Canadian research on compliance costs for individuals

Very little research has been undertaken on the compliance costs for individuals in Canada. A seminal study by François Vaillancourt (1989) estimated the cost to individuals of complying with personal income tax regulations. Using data collected in 1986 through face-to-face surveys of 2,040 residents over the age of 18 in the 10 Canadian provinces, Vaillancourt concluded that individual compliance costs incurred in preparing (sorting documents and gathering information) and completing personal tax returns represented, on average, 2.5% of taxes paid.[7]

---

5 ◆ Indeed, Evans et al., 1996 and 1997, are two of the very few studies available that examine taxes comprehensively and incorporate a standard methodology.

6 ◆ See Appendix 1 (page 28) and Appendix 2 (page 30) for tabular overviews of the research published on this topic. *Nota bene*, however, that the ratios reported in the appendixes are not infallible measures of comparison over time or between countries or taxes. For example, a doubling of the tax rate will have a significant impact on the measures, potentially suggesting that compliance costs compared to revenues have decreased after the rate change when in fact they may still be the same. For that reason, the ratio of compliance costs to GDP is sometimes preferred but that ratio is also subject to the same limitation (GDP can change over time independent of compliance costs).

7 ◆ Since the PIT tax collection system is also used to collect payroll taxes (EI and CPP/QPP premiums) the total revenues used as the denominator in computing this percentage includes PIT, CPP/QPP and EI revenues (Vaillancourt, 1989: 83, note 5).

Vaillancourt (1989) also analyzed the relationship between compliance costs and taxpayer characteristics. He concluded that compliance costs were higher for men than for women, for individuals who are self-employed, and for those with higher levels of education. The author highlighted that most of these variations are due to variations in wages and tax complexity faced by the taxpayer.

International research on compliance costs for individuals
Unfortunately there is also a limited amount of research available outside of Canada about compliance costs for individuals. Several studies have been completed on compliance costs for individuals in the United States.[8] Moody (2005) is the most recent study to examine individual compliance costs in the United States.[9] The author calculated that individual compliance costs of the federal income-tax system were US$110.7 billion in 2005.[10] The author also concluded that compliance costs were regressive, hitting lower-income individuals harder than higher-income individuals. Specifically, individuals with adjusted gross income (AGI) of less than $20,000 incurred compliance costs of 5.9% of their income whereas compliance costs dropped significantly to 0.5% of income for taxpayers earning over $200,000.

Joel Slemrod of the University of Michigan completed a similar study in 2004.[11] The author estimated that total compliance costs for individuals amounted to $85 billion in 2004, which included taxpayer time, preparer fees, and other related expenses, representing 11.1% of personal income-tax revenues.[12] The main reason for the difference in costs expressed in dollars is that Slemrod used a lower value to

---

8 ◆ These studies are highlighted and summarized in the recent GAO report on compliance costs (US GAO, 2005).

9 ◆ In his analysis, the author excluded costs associated with tax planning, tax audits, and litigations.

10 ◆ A previous study by Moody (2002) revealed that compliance costs were $104 billion in 2002.

11 ◆ This study was an update of the research paper completed by Blumenthal and Slemrod in 1992.

12 ◆ Or 1.25% of AGI (available at <http://www.taxpolicycenter.org/TaxFacts/ Tfdb/TFTemplate.cfm?DocID=344&Topic2id=30&Topic3id=32>).

monetize individual taxpayer time than Moody while the difference in ratios is due to the use of a different denominator: income for Moody and taxes for Slemrod.[13]

Most of the remaining research has relied on survey-based work completed in Australia and Europe. For example, two studies by Jeff Pope (Pope et al., 1990; Pope, 1995) as well as a study by Chris Evans and his colleagues (1997) examined personal income-tax compliance costs in Australia. The studies concluded that compliance costs associated with personal income taxes ranged from 4.3% of tax revenues (Evans et al., 1997) to 10.8% of tax revenues (Pope, 1995). As was the case for Canada, the studies found tax compliance costs were higher for the self-employed.[14]

The estimated costs of compliance with personal income taxes as calculated by Pope and Evans were higher than several studies that examined European countries. For example, Delgado and Diaz (1995) analyzed personal income-tax compliance costs in Spain using face-to-face interviews and found that compliance costs represented 3.3% of tax revenues.

The results from a study in Sweden indicated even lower compliance costs. Malmer (1994) examined the compliance costs of personal income taxes. He determined that compliance costs represented 1.0% of tax revenues.

Allers (1994; 1995) examined the compliance costs of personal income taxes and the wealth tax in the Netherlands using face-to-face interviews and drop-off questionnaires. Allers concluded that compliance costs for personal income taxes represented 1.4% of personal income-tax revenues.

Canadian research on compliance costs for business

Recall that the costs incurred by business in complying with tax laws and regulations include both the costs of planning, calculating, and remitting taxes for the business itself as well as the collection and

---

13 ◆ Slemrod monetized taxpayer time using a $20 per hour rate while Moody (2005) used a rate of $39 per hour.

14 ◆ Tran-Nam (2001) found that compliance costs for individuals in Australia were highly regressive. In other words, compliance costs as a percentage of income is higher for low-income earners.

remittance of taxes paid by employees (source deductions) to the government and the provision of information to governments.

More research is available on the compliance costs incurred by businesses both in Canada and internationally than on the compliance costs of individuals. Plamondon (1998) estimated the costs of compliance and administration for Canada's major tax systems for 1996. Using data from Canadian and international research, the author estimated that it cost Canadian businesses between $2.3 billion and $4.5 billion each year to comply with federal and provincial tax regulations, with a midpoint of $3.4 billion. This mid-point represented approximately 0.4% of GDP or 1.5% of tax revenue.

In a study examining both the compliance and administrative costs of payroll and personal income taxes, Vaillancourt (1989) estimated that the compliance costs incurred by employers[15] for personal income taxes and payroll taxes represented 3.5% of taxes collected or 0.5% of GDP.[16]

Vaillancourt (1989) also concluded that these compliance costs, expressed as a percentage of the size of the firm, decreased with firm size. Specifically, an increase in the size of the firm by 1.0% was associated with an increase in compliance costs of between 0.2% to 0.3%, resulting in a decreasing cost-to-size relationship.

Plamondon and Zussman (1998) provide one of the more recent surveys of compliance costs across a number of taxes at both the federal and provincial level.[17] The authors concluded that compliance costs for the GST (federal) were between 3.3% and 6.6% of gross GST revenues. While not as detailed, their cost estimates for provincial sales taxes ranged from relatively low for those jurisdictions that have integrated

---

15 ◆ Data was collected through a mail survey of Canadian employers. In total, 4,196 questionnaires were sent out, of which 9.2% were returned.

16 ◆ Vaillancourt also examined the total compliance and administrative costs of the personal income tax and payroll taxes in Canada. He concluded that the total compliance and administrative costs for personal income taxes and payroll taxes were 6.9% of taxes collected, which he deemed to be in line with international studies (1989: 83).

17 ◆ Interestingly, this study concluded that there were between $171 and $285 million in potential savings from moving to a single-tax administration system.

their provincial sales taxes with the federal GST[18] to relatively high for those provinces that maintain independent sales tax regimes (Veldhuis, 2006). This is an important insight into sources of potential savings, since compliance costs were seen as lower for jurisdictions that had integrated their provincial sales taxes with the federal GST.

Plamondon and Zussman (1998) also provided estimates for compliance costs for corporate income taxes. The authors cite a number of international studies that indicate an average compliance cost of 1% to 2% of taxes remitted for corporate income tax. However, the authors' calculations indicated that the Canadian compliance costs are roughly double those estimates, ranging from roughly 2% to 4% of taxes remitted. The finding that Canadian corporate income taxes impose a high compliance cost on businesses when compared to other jurisdictions may signal the need for reform to preserve competitiveness.

Erard's (1997a) report for the Technical Committee on Business Taxation estimated that the compliance burden for income and capital taxes for large companies in Canada in 1995 was an average of $10.3 to $11.0 million, implying a compliance burden of 4.6% to 4.9% of taxes paid.[19] Plamondon (1998) also completed a survey of compliance costs for small and medium-sized firms. Respondents estimated that they spent $3,829 in compliance costs over a 12-month period, representing an average of 2.6% of sales volume.[20]

Finally, a recent study by the Canadian Federation of Independent Business (CFIB, 2005a) concluded that the average total tax compliance cost for small and medium sized corporations[21] amounted to

---

18 ◆ The study notes that the "incremental compliance costs associated with the QST are minimal" because it is administratively and policy integrated with the federal GST (1998: 765).

19 ◆ The study further noted that the cost of complying with federal and provincial corporate income and capital taxes were substantially higher for firms in the mining, oil, and gas sectors as well as those with foreign operations.

20 ◆ Plamondon's results show that tax compliance costs ranged between 0.2% and 5.7% of sales volume. According to his results, businesses with higher sales volume have decreased compliance costs as a share of sales volume.

21 ◆ Large companies are those with more than 500 employees whereas small and medium-sized firms are defined as those with fewer than 500 employees.

$18,417. The study also calculated and reported the average annual tax-compliance costs on a per-employee basis, ranging from $3,313 for firms with fewer than five employees to $423 for firms with five to 499 employees. In other words, the smaller the business, the higher the tax compliance cost impact per employee.[22, 23]

International research on compliance costs for business

International research supports the Canadian findings. Most of the research on business tax-compliance costs has been undertaken in the United States, Australia, and Europe, especially in the United Kingdom, the Netherlands, and Sweden. As noted earlier, the United States Government Accountability Office (US GAO, 2005) recently concluded a major review of compliance cost studies in the United States.[24] The study reviewed compliance-cost research in the United States for personal income taxes, corporate income taxes, payroll taxes, estate and gift taxes, and excise taxes; and concluded that the lowest compliance-cost estimates for personal and corporate income taxes resulted in costs of $107 billion or roughly 1% of GDP. However, it noted that other studies suggested a higher cost of roughly 1.5% of GDP.

The GAO report includes a number of studies examining business tax compliance costs in the United States. Slemrod (2004) estimated the costs to business of collecting and remitting income and payroll taxes for their employees in 2004 to be approximately $40 billion, which includes corporations and partnerships and covers all costs associated with completing and filing a tax return except postfiling costs such as appeals.

Slemrod and Venkatesh (2002) completed a somewhat narrower examination of business-tax compliance costs for the 2001 tax year

---

22 ◆ Data were reported by firm size using the number of employees to break down the results into four groups. The use of employees as opposed to turnover or sales reflects the information collected in the questionnaire.

23 ◆ The study (CFIB, 2005a) also concluded that differences in rules among provinces increased compliance costs.

24 ◆ The full study is available at <http://www.gao.gov/new.items/d05878.pdf>.

using a comprehensive survey.[25] The study excluded the 1,350 largest corporations in the United States, all businesses with less than $5 million in assets, and all partnerships with less than a requisite number of members. Like Slemrod's 2004 study, this study covered income and payroll taxes, and included all direct and indirect expenses associated with preparing and completing a tax return except for post-filing costs. Not surprisingly given the narrower scope, the overall cost of compliance for businesses was estimated at $22 billion.

Recently, Scott Moody of the US Tax Foundation completed a broad review of tax compliance costs in the United States in 2005 using IRS data. The study included taxpayer and preparer time but excluded other out-of-pocket expenses and post-filing costs. Moody (2005) estimated the cost to businesses in complying with the federal income-tax system in $147.7 billion for fiscal year 2002.[26]

Evans et al. (1996, 1997) have published two of the few studies that attempt to evaluate and calculate compliance costs for all business-related federal taxes. Both studies examined Australia in the 1994/95 period. They estimated that the compliance cost to business, including the self-employed, was about 9.4% of taxes collected or 1.02% of GDP.

Most studies examine specific taxes in order to quantify their compliance costs for business. One can regroup the studies under three headings: corporate income tax, payroll type taxes, and VAT taxes. With respect to the corporate income tax, in a seminal study, Slemrod and Blumenthal (1996) estimated the compliance costs of corporate income taxes for both federal and sub-federal returns. Using a sample of 1,329 large corporations, the authors calculated the compliance costs at 3.2% of revenues collected.

---

25 ◆ Unfortunately, the response rate was rather low (10.25%) and large discrepancies were noted between the results of the survey and actual data. For example, there were large discrepancies between the assets noted by the IRS and what was indicated in the survey responses.

26 ◆ As noted earlier, much of the difference between Moody (2005) and Slemrod (2004) relates to differences in the value used to monetize taxpayer time. Specifically, Moody uses a rate of $47.96 per hour while Slemrod uses a rate of $25 per hour.

Pope (1995) estimated the social compliance burden for corporate income taxes for companies in Australia using data for 1990/91 at approximately 22.9% of revenue collected. Ariff, Ismail, and Loh (1997) provided estimates for compliance costs of corporate income tax in Singapore for 1994/95. The authors' calculations indicated that larger companies (with higher sales) reduced their overall compliance costs as a percentage of sales, which ranged from 0.042% to 0.03%. depending on the size of the firm. A similar study by Chan et al. (1999) for Hong Kong for fiscal 1995 found the usual regressive relationship between company size and compliance costs. They estimated that the compliance cost of corporate income taxes for businesses is about 0.126% of sales turnover.

There have been several studies undertaken on the compliance costs of sales taxes and payroll taxes. For example, Allers (1994, 1995) estimated the costs of compliance and administration for the major tax systems in the Netherlands for 1990. Specifically, he studied the cost for businesses of retaining and remitting payroll taxes, value-added taxes (VAT), and corporate income tax. The author concluded that the average compliance cost represented 4% of taxes collected or 1.5% of GDP. According to the author, the regressivity[27] of compliance costs is confirmed, and the self-employed also typically incurred higher compliance costs.

Similarly, Sandford and Hasseldine (1992) evaluated the compliance costs of employers and business for income tax and the GST in New Zealand for 1989 and 1990. The authors concluded that compliance costs of business taxes were large and cumulative in impact (2.5% of GDP). As in other studies, compliance costs were found to be regressive, falling with disproportionate severity on smaller businesses.

The VAT and source-deducted taxes by businesses in Sweden were studied by Malmer (1995). Using a mail survey, the author estimated the compliance cost of these taxes in 1993 at 1.2% of tax revenues, or equivalent to 0.3% of GDP. Like Allers (1994, 1995), Malmer concluded that compliance costs are regressive. Pope et al. (1993a) studied the burden

---

27 ◆ Compliance costs as percentage of business income are smaller for larger firms.

of employer-collected taxes such as pay-as-you-earn (PAYE), fringe-benefits tax (FBT), prescribed payment system (PPS), and payroll taxes in Australia for the year 1989/90. They estimated the compliance costs of employers' PAYE and payroll tax at 1.4% of revenue yield, while the FBT compliance costs were estimated at 10.9% of revenue yield.

Sandford et al. (1989) evaluated the compliance costs of the value-added tax (VAT) and corporate income tax for 1986 in the United Kingdom. Using a sample of 3,000 businesses, the authors concluded that the average annual compliance costs were 3.7% of VAT revenues collected or the equivalent of 0.7% of taxable sales,[28] implying a compliance burden of 0.24% of GDP.

Collard and Goodwin (1999) studied the compliance costs for employers of pay-as-you-earn (PAYE) and national insurance contributions in the UK in 1995/96. These compliance costs were estimated at 1.3% of tax revenue. Their estimates revealed that compliance costs were highly regressive (bottom 30% pay 75% of compliance costs), and labor costs account for almost half of the compliance costs.

Conclusions

First, more research is needed on the issue of compliance costs, both in Canada and internationally. Second, more standardization is required in the research in order to allow for more accurate inter-tax comparisons to increase understanding of the compliance-cost implications of relying on different taxes. The research reviewed indicates that significant compliance costs are incurred by individuals, families, and businesses in addition to the direct costs of taxation. These costs must be taken into consideration when assessing tax policy and the design of specific taxes. Importantly, a number of scholars and reports have generally concluded that business taxes impose higher compliance costs than individual taxes, and this too should be taken into consideration (US GAO, 2005: 8).

---

28 ◆ Compliance costs as a percentage of business income range from 1.94% for firms with less than £20,500 of business income, to 0.03% for those with more than £10,000,000 of business income. In other words, compliance costs as a percentage of business income are smaller for larger firms.

2 ◆ Estimates of compliance and administration costs in Canada

This section of the study provides estimates of the compliance and administrative costs of the Canadian tax system. Compliance costs are calculated by type of tax while administrative costs are organized by level of government. An overall estimate of the total compliance and administrative costs in Canada for 2005 is provided at the end of the section.

Compliance costs

As noted earlier, compliance costs are those expenses incurred by individuals and businesses to comply with tax regulations. This section presents estimates for compliance costs for personal income taxes, business taxes, and property taxes.

Personal income taxes (PIT)

This section provides estimates of compliance costs for personal income taxes[29] based on two approaches. The first approach uses micro data from various sources (bottom-up approach), while the second uses an aggregate ratio (top-down approach) to calculate the compliance costs of personal income taxes.

Vaillancourt (1989) estimated that the average time to complete a 1985 Canadian (federal and provincial) personal income-tax return was 5.35 hours for all types of returns, regardless of the mode of preparation.[30] This estimate of the total average amount of time required to complete a personal income tax return includes the time spent preparing and sorting documents (2.25 hours), gathering required information (1.01 hours), completing the return (either by self or by an

---

29 ◆ Although personal income tax is largely based on wages and salaries, it also includes income derived from dividends, interest, capital gains, and self-employment.

30 ◆ Note that the estimate does not include the time spent on tax planning or tax appeals. The inclusion of these activities would increase the estimate to 5.55 hours. See Vaillancourt, 1989: table 2.1 (page 26) and table 2.4 (page 36), for more information.

unpaid preparer), and the time spent interacting with paid preparers (if applicable).[31] The average hourly wage for 2005 was $19.09.32,[33] This provides a per-tax-filer estimate of the time cost required to complete a personal income tax return of $102.13 (5.35 hours multiplied by the average hourly wage of $19.09).

According to the Canada Revenue Agency (CRA), there were 23,528,860 tax-filers in 2004 (table 1). This number has been adjusted by 1.6%, which is the average annual growth rate in tax-filers over the last 10 years (from 1995 to 2004) to reflect the expected number of

---

31 ◆ Vaillancourt and Blais (1995) attempted to measure changes in the compliance time associated with personal income taxes over the period from 1971 to 1993. They found a small decrease in the average number of hours required to prepare a personal income tax-form for a typical taxpayer from 1.93 hours in 1985 to 1.76 hours in 1993. However, other data indicates that there may be very little change. For example, table 2.1 on page 28 in Vaillancourt (1989) indicates 0.75 of an hour for preparation of tax documents for all taxpayers. This figure is for all tax-filers compared to 2.28 hours for those preparing reports themselves. This group represented 33.3% of tax-filers (Vaillancourt, 1989: table B-1). A confidential data report from Intuit Canada, a leading tax-preparation group indicated tax-preparation time in 2005 varied from 30 to 60 minutes for the users of its software. Recomputing the 5.35 estimate while assuming that the 2.28 is replaced by 0.75 and taking into account that, according to the data contained in table 3, only one-half of all tax-filers do so electronically with the remaining tax-filers using the standard method yields a time of 5.10 hours. Given the small difference between the two estimates (5.35 versus 5.10), the authors selected the figure based on the larger sample of taxpayers. Note that, while the proliferation of tax software and related technology has certainly increased the accurateness of tax returns, it is unclear whether it has decreased the overall time required to complete returns. For example, such software prompts users to consider deductions and credits that they may not have otherwise considered. In addition, the tax code itself has certainly become more complex since the reforms of the late 1980s, which adds time to completing returns.

32 ◆ According to Statistics Canada's *Canadian Labour Market at a Glance 2005* (Catalogue no. 71-222-XIE), the average hourly wage in Canada was $19.09 before taxes and other deductions.

33 ◆ Pope in C. Sandford (1995) identifies at least six methods by which to value labor time, including self valuation, a reasonable compensation valuation, before-tax wage rate, and after-tax wage rate. For the purposes of our calculation (social costs), before-tax wages were used.

Table 3.1: Tax returns by filing method and agent/author, 2004

	Number of returns (2004)	Percentage	Projections for 2005[1]
Total Returns	23,528,860	1.6%	23,905,322
Taxpayer Filed and Prepared			
Electronic	620,420	2.6%	630,347
Paper (Standard)	8,411,810	35.8%	8,546,399
Tax Preparer Filed			
Electronic	6,639,040	28.2%	6,745,265
Paper (Standard)	3,208,810	13.6%	3,260,151
Tax Preparer Filed, Tax Payer Prepared			
Electronic	3,851,900	16.4%	3,913,530
Paper (Standard)	—	0.0%	—
Filed by Discounter			
Electronic	796,890	3.4%	809,640
Paper (Standard)	—	0.0%	—
Total Electronic	11,908,250	50.6%	12,098,782
Total Paper (Standard)	11,620,620	49.4%	11,806,550

Note 1: The average growth rate over the last 10 years (1995–2004) of 1.6% was used to calculate the expected total number of returns for 2005. The 2004 percentage composition was then applied to the total expected number of returns for 2005.

Sources: Canada Revenue Agency, 2006, Special request (2006-171): Number of Tax Returns by Filing Method and Agent/Author; calculations by the authors.

tax-filers for 2005: 23,905,322 (table 3). The forecast amount of time-based compliance costs for personal income taxes for 2005 is $2.4 billion (table 2).

There are additional costs to consider when developing a micro or bottom-up approach. An estimated $400.2 million to $1.3 billion was paid in 2005 in tax preparer fees (table 2).34 This includes both electronic and standard paper return filing by tax preparers. In addition, a little over 4.5 million Canadian tax-filers completed their personal income tax returns using computer-software. The estimated cost for tax software for 2005 was between $68.2 million and $163.6 million based on average prices ranging from $15 to $36 (table 2).35 Finally, the forecast for 2005 indicates that 809,640 returns were filed by a discounter, with an estimated total cost of $12.1 million (table 2).36

The total estimated compliance costs for personal income taxes, which includes the time associated with completing the tax return, fees paid to preparers, and costs associated with computer software packages is between $2.9 billion and $3.9 billion (table 2).

The second approach is to use established macro or top-down estimates of the compliance costs associated with personal income taxes. Vaillancourt (1989) estimated that compliance costs for personal

---

34 ◆ This number is calculated based on 2004 data from the Canada Revenue Agency, which has been adjusted to reflect expected numbers for 2005. The forecast for 2005 indicates a total of 10,005,416 tax returns completed by tax preparers. See tables 1 and 2 for more information. Two estimates were used to calculate a range of potential costs for tax preparation and completion. The first was based on the average revenues per client served by H&R Block (Canada), one of the country's largest tax-preparer firms. The 2006 annual report of H&R Block indicates a per-client revenue of $39.76 (H&R Block, 2006). The second estimate was based on a confidential report from a professional accounting organization. It indicates the average revenue per client for these services was between $100 and $150 (mid-point of $125 was used).

35 ◆ This figure was calculated based on 2004 data from the Canada Revenue Agency adjusted to reflect expected numbers for 2005. The forecast indicated that 4,543,877 tax returns were completed electronically in 2005. See tables 1 and 2 for more information.

36 ◆ The compliance-cost estimate assumed the lowest cost possible in estimating the fees charged for discounting.

Table 3.2: *Compliance costs for personal income taxes, 2005*

	Lower-bound estimate	Upper-bound estimate
Time Costs, All Returns		
Time required to complete return (hours)	5.35	
Average hourly wage	$19.09	
Number of tax-filers	23,905,322	
Total time cost	**$2,441,486,369**	
Tax Preparer Filed Returns		
Number of returns completed by tax preparers	10,005,416	
Average cost (fee) for preparation	$40	$125
Total preparer costs (fees) paid	$400,216,624	$1,250,676,950
Electronically filed by taxpayer		
Number of returns filed electronically	4,543,877	
Average cost (fee) for preparation	$15	$36
Total preparer costs (fees) paid	$68,158,157	$163,579,576
Filed by a Discounter[1,2]		
Number of returns filed	809,640	
Average cost (fee) for preparation	$15	
Total preparer costs (fees) paid	**$12,144,604**	
Total	$2,922,005,754	$3,867,887,499

Note 1: Users of tax discounters are assumed to have the same costs as all users.

Note 2: The lowest cost estimate was used to proxy the cost for Discounters.

Sources: Canada Revenue Agency, 2007, Special request (2006-171): Number of Tax Returns by Filing Method and Agent/Author; H&R Block, 2006; calculations by the authors.

income taxes represented 3.0%37 of personal income tax revenue or 0.4% of GDP.38 Using these ratios yields a compliance-cost estimate for personal income taxes of between $5.0 billion and $5.5 billion.

The total compliance costs for personal income taxes range from between $2.9 billion (bottom-up approach) to $5.5 billion (top-down approach) depending on the method selected. Total compliance costs for personal income taxes represented between 1.7% and 3.3% of total personal income taxes collected federally and provincially and between 0.2% and 0.4% of GDP in 2005.

Business taxes[39]

This section groups most business taxes together and, like the methodology employed for compliance costs of personal income taxes, relies on two approaches, micro and macro. The micro approach is based on survey work completed by the Canadian Federation of Independent Business (CFIB, 2005a) and research completed by Brian Erard of Carleton University for the Technical Committee on Business Taxation.[40] The CFIB surveyed its members about the total amount of money spent complying with both federal and provincial tax regulations.[41] It specifically differentiated between "outside tax assistance" such as accountants and lawyers and "in-house expenses" such as staff salaries and software. The phrasing of the question was such that overhead costs are more than likely not included. Specifically, no mention was made of overhead either as a generic term or through a list of

---

37 ❖ Appendix 1 indicates an estimate of 2.5% but includes not only personal income taxes but also Unemployment Insurance and Canada and Quebec Pension Plan revenues.

38 ❖ The compliance cost estimate based on GDP is quite similar to the finding for Australia of 0.34% of GDP (Evans, Ritchie, Tran-Nam and Walpole, 1997).

39 ❖ The World Bank carries out international comparisons on the cost of doing business, including the cost of paying and collecting taxes. The study and corresponding data are available at <http://www.doingbusiness.org>.

40 ❖ The studies for the Commission are available at <http://www.fin.gc.ca/tax-study/wpliste.html>.

41 ❖ The survey did not attempt to measure the costs of municipal tax administration, in particular those of property taxes.

indirect expenses such as rent and utilities. The omission, which is a common problem in this kind of study was corrected by adding a standard overhead charge. Research completed by Erard (1997a) provides an estimate for overhead charges (36%)[42] that can be applied to the survey-based results of the CFIB.[43]

Business-tax compliance costs for provincial and federal tax regulations were calculated by applying the compliance costs per employee estimated by the CFIB survey (2005a) by the number of employees in each of the categories (table 3). For example, the CFIB calculated that the compliance cost per employee for firms with five to 19 employees totalled $1,898.[44] That figure was then multiplied by the total number of employees in Canada in firms of that size to arrive at a cost estimate of $3.4 billion for firms with five to 19 employees. This figure was then adjusted to include overhead costs to arrive at a total business tax compliance cost estimate for firms with five to 19 employees of $4.7 billion (table 3).

This calculation was replicated for the four firm sizes covered by the CFIB survey and reported on by Statistics Canada. The authors completed a similar calculation for the final category of employees (500+), which was not covered by the CFIB survey, to arrive at a total estimate of business tax compliance costs for 2005. The total estimated cost of business tax compliance including direct costs, indirect costs, and overheads was $13.0 billion (table 3). This represents 1.0% of GDP in 2005.

The second approach, which uses a macro method to calculate business-tax compliance costs, also relies on research completed by

---

42 ◆ A study of tax compliance costs in the United States by Hall (1993) arrived at a similar overhead charge estimate of 34.0%. See Hall, 1993: table 2, at <http://www.taxfoundation.org/files/6de470dbbb6286da788e6b6f2cc1643a.pdf>.

43 ◆ Erard (1997a) calculated overhead ratios for large corporations, both general and financial, for the Technical Committee on Business Taxation. His conclusion was that overhead expenses (in-house non-personnel) were 36% for large non-financial (general) corporations and 44% for financial corporations. The calculation used in this study has assumed the lower of the two estimates (36%).

44 ◆ This figure has been adjusted to reflect costs in 2005. Specifically, the figure calculated from CFIB in 2004 ($1,857) was adjusted to reflect inflation for 2005.

Table 3.3: Compliance costs for business, 2005

Number of persons employed by enterprise[1]

	0–4	5–19	20–49	50–499	500+	Total
Number of employees (2005)						
	889,148	1,805,841	1,347,166	2,675,322	3,739,536	10,457,013
Compliance costs per employee[2] (CDN$)						
	3,386	1,898	912	432	204	
Total compliance costs before overheads (CDN$)						
	3,010,655,128	3,427,486,218	1,228,615,392	1,155,739,104	762,865,344	9,585,361,186
Imputed overhead (36%) (CDN$)						
	1,083,835,846	1,233,895,038	442,301,541	416,066,077	274,631,524	3,450,730,027
Total compliance costs (CDN$)						
	4,094,490,974	4,661,381,256	1,670,916,933	1,571,805,181	1,037,496,868	13,036,091,213

Note 1: Employment by enterprise size of employment (SEPH) for all employees, unadjusted for seasonal variation, for selected industries classified using the North American Industry Classification System (NAICS), annual persons.

Note 2: CFIB compliance costs data are for 2004 and have been adjusted by the Canadian inflation rate for 2005. Compliance costs per employee for firms with more than 500 employees were assumed by authors given pattern of costs observed for other business size in the CFIB survey (CFIB, 2005a).

Sources: Statistics Canada, 2007, Employment by size, CANSIM Table 281-0042; Statistics Canada, 2006c, Survey of Employment, Payrolls and Hours (SEPH); CFIB (2005a); Erard, 1997a; calculations by the authors.

the Canadian Federation of Independent Business (2005b). This study examined the overall burden of regulations on business in Canada using survey responses of the CFIB's members.[45] The study estimated the total cost of regulations on business at $33 billion in 2005. Applying the ratio of 43% for tax compliance costs compared to total regulatory costs from Cordova-Novion and De Young (2001) results in an estimate of tax compliance costs for business of $14.2 billion in 2005. The 43% ratio is applicable in the Canadian context given the importance of taxes as a source of regulatory burden in Canada. According to the survey respondents, the three most burdensome federal regulations were related to the GST, payroll taxes, and income taxes (CFIB 2005b: 13). In addition, sales taxes were deemed to be the second most burdensome of provincial regulations and property taxes and property assessment regulations were the first and third most costly municipal regulations (CFIB 2005b: 14). Adjusting this macro-based estimate of $14.2 billion to include overhead costs results in a revised compliance cost estimate of $19.3 billion (table 4).

Property taxes
Residential property taxes
According to Statistics Canada (2006b), the number of households in 2005 was 13,014,400 units.[46] We have assumed that, on average, most taxpayers do not appeal their assessment and that a fair and reasonable estimate of the amount of time required to calculate (if applicable), file, and pay personal property taxes ranges between 0.5 hours (low) and 1.0 hour (high) per household.[47] This assumption

---

45 ◆ A total of 5,896 responses were used in calculating the costs of regulations.

46 ◆ According to Statistics Canada's SPSD/M, from which the number of households was extracted, the definition of a household is: "The household (e.g. single family dwelling, townhouse, apartment unit, etc.) is the basic unit of the Survey of Labour and Income Dynamics, the unit on which the SPSD is essentially based. The definition of household is keyed to dwelling location, and does not consider the interrelationships of its members beyond the fact that they live in the same unit."

47 ◆ The authors readily acknowledge that many property owners spend little or no time on personal property taxes as it is automated with financial institutions.

Table 3.4: Total compliance costs, 2005 (CDN$)

	Lower-bound estimate	Upper-bound estimate
Personal income taxes	2,922,005,754	5,474,904,000
Business taxes	13,036,091,213	19,300,000,000
Property taxes, personal	124,222,448	248,444,896
Property taxes, business[1]	100,058,899	—
Total compliance costs	16,182,378,313	25,023,348,896

Note 1: Business property taxes are removed from the aggregate macro-estimate because they are included in the estimate of business tax compliance costs.

Sources: see tables 1, 2, and 3; calculations by the authors.

leads to an estimate of between $124.2 and $248.4 million for the cost of compliance with personal property taxes (table 4).[48] Both the lower- and upper-bound estimates are included in the overall calculation of compliance costs (table 4).

Business property taxes

According to Statistic Canada's Small Business Research and Policy group (Statistics Canada, 2006c) there were 1,048,286 business establishments in Canada in 2005.[49] This figure includes only those establishments defined as Employer Businesses, which means that they have employees. It purposely excludes individuals and family members since these types of establishments are unlikely to pay business property taxes.

However, some property owners receive more than one bill per year (3 in Montreal for example). In addition, some personal property owners appeal their assessments, which means additional time and expenses. Finally, some individuals may be operating businesses out of their homes and thus may incur higher compliance costs.

48 ◆ This estimate uses the average national hourly wage of $19.09 per hour.

49 ◆ The data is available from Statistics Canada's Strategis Group, which includes the Small Business Research and Policy Group: <http://strategis.ic.gc.ca/epic/site/sbrp-rppe.nsf/en/rd01832e.html>.

If we assume a range of five hours (low) to 10 hours (high) for compliance time[50] for business property taxes and use the national hourly wage rate ($19.09), we arrive at an estimate of between $100.1 million and $200.1 million for compliance costs for business property taxes (table 4). This is higher than the typical costs but takes into account implicitly the fact that some businesses appeal their tax bills. The lower-bound estimate is included in the calculation (table 4) for total compliance costs while the upper-bound estimate is excluded since it is included in the overall upper-bound business-tax compliance cost estimate.[51]

The overall estimate for compliance costs for property taxes, using explicit costs for both personal and business property taxes for 2005 is between $224.3 and $448.5 million depending on the estimate used for the number of hours required to complete property taxes each year.[52] According to Statistics Canada, total property taxes in 2005 were approximately $41.1 billion.[53] Thus, property-tax compliance costs represent roughly between 0.5% and 1.1% of property taxes collected. This is a reasonable estimate given the evidence available on compliance costs of other taxes in Canada and abroad.[54]

Total compliance costs
The data and calculations contained in tables 1, 2, and 3 are combined to determine an overall cost of tax compliance in Canada in 2005

---

50 ◆ This estimate is based on the authors' experience and interpretation of past research. It includes all aspects of tax compliance including planning, preparing, organizing, and remitting tax payments.

51 ◆ The CFIB (2005b) report included property taxes in the calculation of the overall burden of regulations on business in Canada.

52 ◆ Please note that the upper bound estimate for business property taxes of $200.1 million is excluded from the overall calculation and tables 4 and 6 because business property taxes are included in the upper-bound estimate of overall business tax compliance costs.

53 ◆ CANSIM table 385-0001, all governments.

54 ◆ Note that we have been unable to find any other evidence on the compliance costs of property taxes in Canada. In addition, none of the four external referees were aware of any additional research or evidence.

of between \$16.2 billion and \$25.0 billion (table 4). This represents between 3.0% and 4.7% of total federal, provincial and local total revenues and between 1.2% and 1.8% of GDP in 2005.

Administrative costs

As defined previously, administrative costs are incurred by governments in order to collect taxes and enforce tax regulations. These costs include collecting, administering, and managing the tax collection system itself.

The administrative costs incurred by governments in Canada to maintain and administer the tax collection system were documented by examining government financial statements (Public Accounts) as well as departmental reports. In addition, the authors examined reports by municipalities and tax assessment agencies in order to collect a broad spectrum of potential and actual administrative costs.[55]

Administrative costs incurred by the Canada Revenue Agency, which are readily available in the federal Public Accounts, including the costs of collecting federal personal income taxes, corporate income taxes, the goods and services tax (GST), the harmonized provincial GST, payroll taxes such as employment insurance, excise duties, provincial personal income taxes (except Quebec) and provincial corporate income taxes (except for Alberta, Ontario, and Quebec). The administrative costs for these taxes amounted to \$3.7 billion in 2005 (table 5).

Administrative costs for a host of taxes collected provincially, which include British Columbia, Alberta, Saskatchewan, Manitoba, Ontario, Québec and the Atlantic provinces, were all found in provincial sources, including both provincial Public Accounts and provincial treasury reports.

Finally, the administrative costs for property taxes were set at 2% of taxes based on a review of the cost of collecting property

---

55 ◆ Vaillancourt reports that the costs of central agencies and courts are negligible with respect to the PIT system: "less than 1%" (1989: 74).

Table 3.5: Administrative costs, 2005 (CDN$ millions)

Government	Amount	Taxes covered
Federal: Canada Revenue Agency[1]	3,700	Federal PIT, CIT, GHST/HST, payroll taxes, excises taxes & duties federally collected provincial PIT and CIT
Alberta	55	Provincial CIT, some excises
British Columbia	41	Sales tax, excises
Ontario	460	CIT, sales tax, excises, payroll tax
Québec	870	PIT, CIT, QST/GST, excises, payroll tax
Manitoba	16	Sales tax, excises
Saskatchewan	11	Sales tax, excises
Atlantic provinces(estimated)	40	Excises and sales in PEI
Municipalities and school boards[1]	600	Property taxes
Total	5,793	

Note 1: includes payment to Revenu Québec for GST collection; said amount not included in Revenu Québec costs.

Note 2: For municipal costs, we use information for Montréal and British Columbia as follows. **Montréal**: Property tax revenues 2007: $1,379,257,000 (Ville de Montreal, 2007, p. 258, table 70); Budget of the valuation unit for 2007: $21,437,000 (Ville de Montreal, 2007, p. 271, table 78); ratio is 1.5%; ◆ **British Columbia**: Amount spent 2005: $70,682,000 (British Columbia Assessment Authority, 2005, p. 71); Revenue 2005: $2,700,000,000 municipal property tax (p. 15), or ratio of 2.5%, or $5,000,000,000 total; 1.4% ratio. ◆ These are large organizations; we assumed higher costs overall to take into account the size of various municipalities in Canada.

Sources: Public Accounts of the federal and provincial governments.

Provincial Administrative Costs ◆ **Québec**: Revenu Québec, 2005, Comptes publics du Québec 2005-2006, p. 2–172, <http://www.finances.gouv.qc.ca/documents/Comptespublics/fr/vol2-2005-2006.pdf>; ◆ **Ontario**: Ministry of Finance, 2006, The Estimates 2006-2007, Tax revenue (Vote 743 Main estimates), <http://www.fin.gov.on.ca/english/budget/estimates/2006-07/volume1/mof_743.html>; ◆ **Alberta**: Alberta Finance, 2005, Alberta Finance Annual Report 2005-2006, Consolidated Statements of Operations, p. 51 <http://www.finance.gov.ab.ca/publications/annual_repts/finance/annrep06/far002.pdf>; ◆ **British Columbia**: Ministry of Small Business and Revenue, 2005, Annual Service Plan Reports 2005/06, Revenue Programs, <http://www.bcbudget.gov.bc.ca/Annual_Reports/2005_2006/sbr/Service_Delivery_and_Core_Business_Areas.htm>; ◆ **Manitoba**: Manitoba Finance, 2005, Annual report 2005-2006, Taxation Division, p.37-45, <http://www.gov.mb.ca/finance/annualrep/2005_06/finance.pdf>; ◆ **Saskatchewan**: Saskatchewan Finance, 2005, 2005-2006 Annual Report, p.25, <http://www.gov.sk.ca/finance/annreport/annualreport20052006.pdf>.

Municipal Administrative Costs ◆ **Montréal**: Ville de Montreal, 2007, Budget du conseil d'agglomeration 2007, <http://ville.montreal.qc.ca/pls/portal/docs/page/service_fin_fr/media/documents/budget-2007-14-cag-activites.pdf>; ◆ **British Columbia**: British Columbia Assessment Authority, 2005, 2005 Annual Report, <http://www.bcassessment.bc.ca/pdf/publications/reports/2005_annual_report.pdf>.

taxes in Montreal and British Columbia.[56] The total estimate for administrative costs associated with taxation in Canada for 2005 is \$5.8 billion (table 5).[57]

Plamondon et al. (1997) offer an alternative estimate for administration costs.[58] They calculated administrative costs to be \$2.2 billion in 1995, which adjusted for inflation, results in an estimate for 2005 of \$2.7 billion. Please note that this estimate implicitly assumes no changes upwards or downwards in the complexity or costs associated with tax collection and management of tax regulations on the part of government. It represents our lower-bound estimate of potential administrative costs in Canada for 2005.

Conclusion

Table 6 summarizes the total compliance and administrative costs estimated for Canada for 2005. In total, tax compliance costs range from \$16.2 billion to \$25.0 billion depending on the methodology employed. Administrative costs in Canada in 2005 were estimated at between \$2.7 billion and \$5.8 billion. Thus, total compliance and administrative costs in Canada for 2005 range between \$18.9 billion and \$30.8 billion (table 6). This represents between 3.5% and 5.8% of total federal, provincial and local revenues and between 1.4% and 2.3% of GDP in 2005.

---

56 ◆ Specifically, an author discussed this issue with an official in the Finance Department of Montreal, reviewed their budgets and assessed the costs of operation of the property tax assessment agency in British Columbia.

57 ◆ Two biases in the calculations should be noted. First, the calculations do not include the costs of the justice system and of central services. Vaillancourt (1989) found these costs to amount to roughly 2% of the direct costs of collecting federal personal income and payroll taxes. Second, the calculations may inadvertently include some spending by provincial finance departments that is not directly linked to collecting and managing the tax system. It seems reasonable to expect these two biases, one positive and one negative, and neither substantial, to cancel one another out.

58 ◆ CFIB estimated that the Canada Revenue Agency's operating costs amounted to 2.06% of tax revenues collected in 2003/04 (2005a: 10).

Table 3.6: Total compliance and administrative costs, 2005 (CDN$)

	Lower-bound estimate	Upper-bound estimate[1]
Personal income taxes, individual	2,922,005,754	5,474,904,000
Business taxes	13,036,091,213	19,300,000,000
Property taxes[2]	224,281,347	248,444,896
Total compliance costs	16,182,378,313	25,023,348,896
Administrative costs[3]	2,690,000,000	5,793,300,000
Total compliance and administrative costs	18,872,378,313	30,816,648,896
Per capita (32,271,000)	$585	$955

Note 1: Most of the upper bound estimates were derived from macro estimates.

Note 2: The difference in compliance costs for property taxes is due to the inclusion of business property taxes in the macro method in business taxes generally and in the use of different estimates for residential property taxes.

Note 3: Lower bound estimate is derived from an inflation-adjusted estimate based on Plamondon's work (1998).

Sources: Tables 1, 4, and 5; calculations by the authors; Statistics Canada, Income and Expenditure Accounts Division, 2006.

To place the aggregate figures in context for readers, per-capita and tax-filer estimates were also calculated (table 6). Each Canadian incurred compliance and administrative costs associated with the country's tax system in 2005 of between $585 and $955.

The results presented above and throughout this paper show that individuals and businesses incur significant costs to comply with the tax system and that governments expend significant resources administering the tax system. It is, therefore, important that better research be undertaken regarding tax compliance and administrative costs.

Recommendations

Although improving the compliance and administrative costs was not a central goal of this study, there are a number of specific measures that could be taken to reduce such costs. Five are presented below for interest; this list is not, by any means, exhaustive and, in fact, includes only some of the more simple and straightforward reforms available to policy-makers.

1 ◆ *Harmonize provincial sales taxes*
Harmonizing provincial sales taxes with the federal sales tax (GST) is one method that reduces compliance costs for business and administrative costs for government (Plamondon and Zussman, 1998). Harmonizing the five provincial sales taxes that are currently independent from the federal GST (British Columbia, Saskatchewan, Manitoba, Ontario, and Prince Edward Island) would result in reduced paper work and administration for businesses and lower collection costs for governments.

2 ◆ *Explore tax collection agreements*
Exploring the possibility of tax collection agreements (TCA), such as the one now in place between Ontario and the federal government for corporate income taxes, could result in additional savings in administrative costs. These costs have already been lowered by the existence of various tax collection agreements with respect to the provincial personal income tax (9 provinces) and corporate income tax (7 provinces).

3 ◆ *Improve technology at the Canada Revenue Agency*
Improved and more advanced technology at the Canada Revenue Agency might also bring about improved private-sector and public-sector systems that reduce compliance and administrative costs. Specifically, improving technology at CRA could allow more efficient private-sector technologies to emerge while improving efficiency at CRA itself.

4 ◆ *Raise the GST threshold*

Modifying (raising) the GST threshold, which has not been adjusted since implementation, may alleviate some of the recognized problems regarding compliance costs for VAT-type taxes relative to firm size.[59]

5 ◆ *Eliminate complex tax policies*

More generally, reducing or eliminating tax policies that add complexity to the tax system such as special preferences, multiple tax rates, and the number of taxes collected, to name a few would also reduce the complexity and thus the compliance and administrative costs of the tax system.

---

59 ◆ We must note, however, that many businesses with sales below the threshold already voluntarily register for the GST because it entitles them to claim GST input credits on their capital purchases. See Keen and Mintz, 2004 for an interesting discussion of the optimal GST threshold.

Appendix 3.1: *Studies of the compliance costs for individuals, 1985–2006*

Tax; survey type (year of data)	Size of sample; type of respondents	Response rate
Vaillancourt,1989; Canada		
PIT; face to face interviews (1986)	2,040 individuals	100%
Moody, 2005; United States		
Data from the Internal Revenue Agency (IRS)	—	—
Slemrod, 2004; United States		
Update of Blumenthal and Slemrod, 1992	—	—
Pope, Fayle and Duncanson,1990; Pope, 1995; Australia		
PIT postal survey (1988)	6,737 individuals	16.3%
Evans, Ritchie, Tran-Nam and Walpole, 1997; Australia		
PIT postal survey (1995)	1,996 tapayers	50%
Blumenthal and Slemrod, 1992; Minnesota, United States		
PIT postal survey (1989-1990)	2,000 individuals	43.2%
Delgado and Diaz, 1992; Spain		
PIT face to face interviews (1989)	2,355 individuals out of 2,500 agreeing to be interviewed	100%
Malmer, 1994; Sweden		
PIT postal survey (1992)	12,000 individuals	67%
Allers, 1994, 1995; Netherlands		
PIT and wealth tax	24,920 individuals contacted	44%

Sources: Vaillancourt, 1999; compiled by authors.

Average compliance costs	Conclusions
2.5 % of tax revenue	Costs increase, then decrease, with age; increase with schooling.
Ranges from 0.45% to 5.87% of adjusted gross income (AGI)	Compliance costs for individuals amounted to $110.7 billion; are highly regressive, hitting lower-income individuals harder than higher-income individuals.
11.1% of personal income tax revenue	Compliance costs for individuals rose from 8.5% in 1995 to 11.1% of personal income tax revenue in 2004.
4.3 to 10.8 % of tax revenue	Costs increase with tax complexity and are higher for the self employed
4.0 % of tax revenue; 0.34% of GDP	Self-employed individuals face higher compliance costs
$353.7 per respondent in 1989	Low- and high-income households have higher compliance costs; costs increase with schooling and are higher for the self employed.
3.3 % of tax revenue	Most taxpayers use outside help with better educated ones using it less; monetary cost is regressive (fixed amount/income)
1.0 % of tax revenue	Self-employed individuals or those selling assets face higher compliance costs
1.4 % of PIT revenue	Income tax + compliance time increases with age, education and income

Appendix 3.2: Studies of the compliance costs for businesses, 1985–2006

Tax; survey type (year of data)	Size of sample; type of respondents	Response rate	Average compliance costs as % of selected indicator
Brown and Vaillancourt, 1986; Canada			
Federal sales tax; face-to-face for large firms (1985); postal survey (1985)	36 large manufacturing firms; 1600 small manufacturing firms; sample from revenue Canada list	60% 11%	0.67% of revenue of federal sales tax for large firms; 2,775% for small firms
Vaillancourt, 1989; Canada			
Personal income tax and payroll taxes; postal survey (1986)	4,196 employers; sample from Dunn and Bradstreet list	9%	0.1% of before-tax entreprise income; 3.5% of taxes
Erard, 1997a; Canada			
CIT and capital taxes; postal survey (1996)	250 firms members of Tax Executive Institute	24%	0.03% gross receipts; CDN$97 per employee
Plamondon, 1997; Canada			
All taxes; phone survey (1997)	3,082 small entreprises; sales <5 millions	41%	2.55% of sales
CFIB, 2005a; Canada			
All taxes web survey (2004)	Small and medium businesses (less than 500 employees)	1,935	18,417 per small and medium enterprise
Sandford, Godwin and Hardwick, 1989: United Kingdom			
Value added tax(VAT); corporate income tax (CIT); postal survey (1987)	3,000 businesses; sample from inland Revenue	23%	3.69% of VAT collected; 0.69% of taxable sales

Costs as % of country output	Compliance costs by size of business, smallest and largest size category	Conclusions
0.16% of GNP	Costs over taxable sales: smallest 1/3: 0.12; largest 1/3: 0.055	Compliance costs as % of business income are smaller for larger firms and higher with the degree of complexity (number of rates, exemptions …)
0.54% of GDP	Cost over gross income; smallest 1/3: 3.36; largest 1/3: 0.64	Compliance costs as % of business income are smaller for larger firms. Using alternative measures of size (number of employees or tax documents does not change this finding)
n/a	—	Natural resources sector incurs higher costs; costs increase with the number of provinces where CIT is paid
n/a	Cost/business income: less than $50,000: 5.7; $2–5 million: 0.2	Sales taxes generate more compliance costs issues than others
n/a	$ per employee: 0–4 employees: $3,313; 50–499 employees: $423	Differences in rules between provinces increases compliance costs
0.24% of GDP	Cost/taxable sales: less than 20,500: 1.94; above 10,000,000: 0.03	Compliance costs as % of business income are smaller for larger firms; large firms gain from improved cash flow

Appendix 3.2 (cont'd): Studies of the compliance costs for businesses, 1985–2006

Tax; survey type (year of data)	Size of sample; type of respondents	Response rate	Average compliance costs as % of selected indicator
Sandford and Hasseldine, 1992; Hasseldine, 1995; New Zealand			
Pay as you earn (P.A.Y.E.); fringe benefits tax (FBT); Goods and Services tax (GST-VAT), CIT; Postal surveys of independent samples (1991)	4,743 employers; 9,541 businesses; sample from Inland Revenue	40%; 31%	1.92% of P.A.Y.E. revenue; 1.73% of FBT revenue; 7.3% of GST revenue
Pope, Fayle, and Chen, 1993a, 1993b, 1994; Pope, 1995; Australia			
P.A.Y.E., FBT, PPS (Prescribed Payment System); postal survey (1989/1990); wholesales tax (WST); postal survey (1990/1991); CIT postal survey (1990/1991)	2,739 entreprises; 2,467 entreprises; 2,531 entreprises; sample from phone book	27%; 24%: 34%	13.8% of PIT and CIT revenues; 1.9% of WST revenue
Allers, 1994, 1995; Netherlands			
Taxes collected or paid by businesses (payroll taxes, VAT,CIT,PAYE); postal survey (1990)	5,393 entreprises; stratified sample from chamber of commerce list	20%	4% of tax revenue
Malmer, 1994; Sweden			
VAT and source deducted taxes by businesses; postal survey (1993)	9,361; phone filtered sample based on offical lists (50,499 employees)	64%	1.2% of tax revenue
Blumenthal and Slemrod, 1996; United States			
CIT federal and state; postal survey (1992)	1,672 large enterprises in Coordinated Examination Program of the IRS;1329 active	28%	3.2% of total CIT; 2.6% of federal CIT; 5.6% of state CIT

Costs as % of country output	Compliance costs by size of business, smallest and largest size category	Conclusions
2.5% of GDP for taxes studied	Cost/business income; less than $30,000: 13.4; more than $50 million: 0.03	Compliance costs as % of business income are smaller for larger firms; simpler tax procedures are associated with lower complaince costs
2.1% of GDP for taxes studied	Cost/business income (PAYE): less than $500,000: 4.0; $5–10 million: 0.2 :0.4	Compliance costs as % of business income are smaller for larger firms; CIT is an important source of compliance costs
1.5% of GDP	—	Compliance costs as % of business income are smaller for larger firms; variations in compliance costs by sector are explained mainly by differences in firm size but the retail sector exhibits higher costs for all sizes of firms
0.3% of GDP	—	Small enterprises (measured by number of employees) have substantially higher compliance costs than large ones; VAT compliance costs are double those of other taxes
n/a	Costs/sales: less than 250,000: 0.46; more than 5,000,000: 0.05	Compliance costs as % of business income are smaller for larger firms; primary sector firms incur higher compliance costs

Appendix 3.2 (cont'd): Studies of the compliance costs for businesses, 1985–2006

Tax; survey type (year of data)	Size of sample; type of respondents	Response rate	Average compliance costs as % of selected indicator
Ariff, Zubaidah, and Loh, 1997; Singapore			
CIT postal survey (1995)	234 firms on Singapore stock exchange	26%	0.042–0.03% of turnover (1994/1995)
Evans, Ritchie, Tran Nam, and Walpole, 1997: Australia			
All federal taxes; postal survey (1995)	8,039 sole traders (self-employed) and entreprises	31%	9.8% of tax revenues
Chan et al., 1999; Hong Kong			
CIT; postal survey (1995/1996)	58/75/496 firms on Hong Kong stock exchange	15.10%	0.126% of sales
Collard and Goodwin, 1999; United Kingdom			
PAYE national insurance, (1995/1996); postal survey	5,195 employers, provided by Inland Revenue	29.20%	1.3% of revenue
Hasseldine and Hansford, 2002; United Kingdom			
VAT ; postal survey (2000)	6,232 business taxpayers	23%	
Selmrod and Venkatesh, 2002; United States			
Business tax compliance costs; survey	Excludes the largest 1,350 corporations, all businesses with less than $5 million in assets, and all partnerships with less than a certain number of partners.	10.25%	Compliance burden was estimated in $22 billions

Costs as % of country output	Compliance costs by size of business, smallest and largest size category	Conclusions
n/a	Costs /turnover: smallest: 0.4; largest: 0.08	Lower reliance on external assistance reduced costs as evidenced in large firms
1.94% of GDP	Cost/business income: smallest : 3.4; largest: 0.18	P.A.Y.E. et WST have lower costs than PPS or FBT
n/a	Cost /sales: less than 100,000: 5.41; more than 5,500,000: 0.21	Higher compliance costs in Hong Kong relative to Singapore may be related to lower administrative costs in Hong Kong; more reliance on external advisers than in other countries is observed
n/a	Size band (employees) ratio to revenue: 1–4: 7.9; 5,000+: 0.14	A higher turnover in staff (joiners/leavers) increases costs; 75% of costs incurred by the smallest 30% taxpayers; sufficiently large employers can reduce costs with more technologically advanced method
		Increased compliance costs are associated with increased turnover, newly registered businesses, increased complexity and perceived psychological costs

Appendix 3.2 (cont'd): Studies of the compliance costs for businesses, 1985–2006

Tax; survey type (year of data)	Size of sample; type of respondents	Response rate	Average compliance costs as % of selected indicator
Slemrod, 2004; United States			
Update of Slemrod and Blumental, 1996	Covers all corporations and partnerships	—	Compliance costs were estimated in $40 billions, which represents 23.7% of corporate tax collected.
Moody, 2005; United States			
Data from the Internal Revenue Agency (IRS)	—	—	Compliance costs for businesses were estimated at $148 billion (including sole proprietors). Businesses bear 56% of total compliance costs.

Sources: Vaillancourt, 1999; compiled by authors.

Costs as % of country output	Compliance costs by size of business, smallest and largest size category	Conclusions
	Compliance costs for corporations has doubled since 1995.	

References

Allers, Maarten A. (1994). *Administrative and Compliance Costs of Taxation and Public Transfers in the Netherlands.* Groningen theses in economics, management and organization. Wolters-Noordhoff.

Allers, Maarten A. (1995). Tax Compliance Costs in the Netherlands. In Cedric Sandford, ed., *Tax Compliance Costs: Measurement and Policy* (Fiscal Publications): 173–95.

Alm, James (1988). Compliance Costs and the Tax Avoidance-Tax Evasion Decision. *Public Finance Quarterly* 16, 1: 31–66.

Alm, James (1996). What Is an "Optimal" Tax System? *National Tax Journal* 49, 1: 117–34.

Ariff, Mohammed, Ismail Zubaidah, and A. Loh (1997). Compliance Costs of Corporate Income Taxation in Singapore. *Journal of Business Finance and Accounting* 24, 9-10: 1253–68.

Bannock, Graham (2001). Can Small Scale Surveys of Compliance Costs Work? In C. Evans, J. Pope and J. Hasseldine, eds., *Taxation Compliance Costs: A Festschrift for Cedric Sandford* (Prospect Media): 87–98.

Bird, Richard M. (1982). The Costs of Collecting Taxes: Preliminary Reflections on the Uses and Limits of Cost Studies. *Canadian Tax Journal* 30, 6: 860–65.

Blumenthal, Marsha, and Joel Slemrod (1992). The Compliance Cost of the US Individual Income Tax System: A Second Look after Tax Reform. *National Tax Journal* 45, 2: 185–202.

Brown, J., and Francois Vaillancourt (1986). *The Administrative and Compliance Costs of the Federal Sales Tax System.* A study prepared for the Department of Finance. Department of Finance, Government of Canada.

Canadian Federation of Independent Business (2005a). *Canada's Revenue Agency Five Years After*. <http://www.cfib.ca/research/reports/crareport.pdf>.

Canadian Federation of Independent Business (2005b). *Rated "R": Prosperity Restricted by Red Tape*. <http://www.cfib.ca/research/reports/RatedR.pdf>.

Chan, S.Y.S., Daniel Cheung, Mohammed Ariff, and A. Loh (1999). Compliance Costs of Corporate Taxation in Hong Kong. *International Tax Journal* 25, 4: 42–68.

Clemens, Jason, and Niels Veldhuis (2005). *Growing Small Businesses in Canada: Removing the Tax Barrier*. The Fraser Institute.

Clemens, Jason, Niels Veldhuis, and Milagros Palacios (2007). *Tax Efficiency: Not All Taxes Are Created Equal*. The Fraser Institute.

Cnossen, Sijbren (1994). Administrative and Compliance Costs of the VAT: A Review of the Evidence. *Tax Notes International* 8 (June 20): 1649–68.

Collard, David, and Michael Goodwin (1999). Compliance Costs for Employers: UK PAYE and National Insurance, 1995–1996. *Fiscal Studies* 20, 4: 423–49.

Cordova-Novion, Cesar, and Casandra de Young (2001). The OECD PUMA Multi Country Business Survey – Benchmarking the Regulatory and Business Environment. In C. Evans, J. Pope, and J. Hasseldine, eds., *Taxation Compliance Costs: A Festschrift for Cedric Sandford* (Prospect Media): 205–28.

Delgado, Maria Luisa, and Consuelo Diaz (1995). Personal Income Tax Compliance Costs in Spain. In Cedric Sandford, ed., *Tax Compliance Costs: Measurement and Policy* (Fiscal Publications): 226–62.

Erard, Brian (1997a). *The Income Tax Compliance Burden on Canadian Big Business.* Working Paper 97-2 (April). Technical Committee on Business Taxation.

Erard, Brian (1997b). *The Income Tax Compliance Burden on Small and Medium-sized Canadian Businesses.* Working Paper 97-12 (October). Technical Committee on Business Taxation.

Evans, Chris (2003). Studying the Studies: An Overview of Recent Research into Taxation Operating Costs. *eJournal of Tax Research* 1, 1: 64–92.

Evans, Chris, Jeff Pope, and John Hasseldine, eds. (2001). *Taxation Compliance Costs: A Festschrift for Cedric Sandford.* Prospect Media.

Evans, Chris, Katherine Ritchie, Binh Tran-Nam, and Michael Walpole (1996). *A Report into the Incremental Costs of Taxpayer Compliance.* Commonwealth Information Services.

Evans, Chris, Katherine Ritchie, Binh Tran-Nam, and Michael Walpole (1997). *A Report into Taxpayer Costs of Compliance.* Commonwealth Information Services.

Friedman, David, and Joel Waldfogel (1995). The Administrative and Compliance Cost of Manual Highway Toll Collection Evidence from Massachusetts and New Jersey. *National Tax Journal* 48, 2: 217–28.

Gunz, Sally, Alan Macnaughton, and Karen Wensley (1995). Measuring the Compliance Costs of Tax Expenditures: The Case of Research and Development Incentives. *Canadian Tax Journal* 43, 6: 2008–34.

Guyton, John L., John F. O'Hare, and Michael P. Stavrianos (2003). Estimating the Compliance Cost of the U.S. Individual Income Tax. *National Tax Journal* 56, 3: 673–88.

H & R Block (2006). *Annual Report for H & R Block*. H & R Block.

Hall, Arthur (1993). *The High Cost of Tax Compliance for U.S. Business*. Special report 25 (November). Tax Foundation.

Hansford, Ann, John Hasseldine, and Carol Howard (2003). Factors Affecting the Costs of UK VAT Compliance for Small and Medium Sized Enterprises. *Environment and Planning C: Government and Policy* 21, 4: 479–92.

Hasseldine, John (1995). Compliance Costs of Business Taxes in New-Zealand. In Cedric Sandford, ed., *Tax Compliance Costs: Measurement and Policy* (Fiscal Publications): 126–41.

Hasseldine, John (2001). Linkages between Compliance Costs and Taxpayer Compliance Research. In C. Evans, J. Pope, and J. Hasseldine, eds., *Taxation Compliance Costs: A Festschrift for Cedric Sandford* (Prospect Media): 3–14.

Hasseldine, John, and Ann Hansford (2002). The Compliance Burden of the VAT: Further Evidence from the UK. *Australian Tax Forum* 17, 4: 369–88.

Hendricks, Kenneth, Raphael Amit, and Diana Whistler (1997). *Business Taxation of Small and Medium-Sized Enterprises in Canada*. Working Paper 91-11. Prepared for the Technical Committee on Business Taxation. Department of Finance, Government of Canada.

Keen, Michael, and Jack Mintz (2004): The Optimal Threshold for a Value-Added Tax. *Journal of Public Economics* 88 3-4 (March): 559–76.

Kesselman, Jonathan R. (1994). Compliance, Enforcement, and Administrative Factors in Improving Tax Fairness. In Allan M. Maslove, ed., *Issues in the Taxation of Individuals* (University of Toronto Press): 62–84.

Kesselman, Jonathan R. (1997). Policy Implications of Tax Evasion and the Underground Economy. In Owen Lippert and Michael Walker, eds., *The Underground Economy: Global Evidence of Its Size and Impact* (Fraser Institute): 293–317.

Malmer, Hakan (1995). The Swedish Tax Reform in 1990-1991 and Tax Compliance Costs in Sweden. In Cedric Sandford, ed., *Tax Compliance Costs: Measurement and Policy* (Fiscal Publications): 226–62.

Moody, Scott (2002). *The Cost of Complying with the Federal Income Tax*. Special Report 112. Tax Foundation.

Moody, Scott (2005). *The Cost of Complying with the Federal Income Tax*. Special Report 138. Tax Foundation.

National Audit Office (1994). *Cost to Business of Complying with VAT Requirement*. House of Commons Paper 319. HMSO.

Plamondon & Associates Inc. (1993). *GST Compliance Costs for Small Business in Canada. A Study for the Department of Finance, Tax Policy*. Department of Finance, Government of Canada.

Plamondon & Associates Inc. (1996). *Compliance Issues: Small Business and the Corporate Income Tax System*. Technical Committee on Business Taxation.

Plamondon, Robert E. (1998). *Cutting the Costs of Tax Collection Down to Size: Estimating the Magnitude of Compliance and Administrative Costs of Canada's Tax System—and the Impact of Single Administration*. Public Policy Forum (January). A report prepared for Revenue Canada. <http://www.ppforum.com/common/assets/publications/en/ow_p_01_1998_fr.pdf>.

Plamondon, Robert E., and David Zussman (1998). *The Compliance Costs of Canada's Major Tax Systems and the Impact of Single Administration. Canadian Tax Journal* 46, 4: 761–85.

Pope, Jeff (1995). The Compliance Costs of Major Taxes in Australia. In Cedric Sandford, ed., *Tax Compliance Costs: Measurement and Policy* (Fiscal Publications): 101–25.

Pope, Jeff (2001). Estimating and Alleviating the Goods and Service Tax Compliance Cost Burden upon Small Business. *Revenue Law Journal* 11: 6–22.

Pope, Jeff, Richard Fayle, and Dong-Ling Chen (1993a). *The Compliance Costs of Employment-Related Taxation.* Research Studies Series 17. Australian Tax Research Foundation.

Pope, Jeff, Richard Fayle, and Dong-Ling Chen (1993b). *The Compliance Costs of the Wholesale Sales Tax.* Research Studies Series 19. Australian Tax Research Foundation.

Pope, Jeff, Richard Fayle, and Dong-Ling Chen (1995). *The Compliance Costs of Companies' Income Taxation.* Research Studies Series 23. Australian Tax Research Foundation.

Pope, Jeff, Richard Fayle, and Mike Duncanson (1990). *The Compliance Costs of Personal Income Taxation in Australia, 1986/87.* Research Studies Series 9. Australian Tax Research Foundation.

Poutziouris Panikkos, Francis Chittenden, and Nicos Michaelas (2001). The Tax Burden of Direct Taxes and Compliance Costs of the UK Small Company Sector – A Simulation Model. In C. Evans, J. Pope, and J. Hasseldine, eds., *Taxation Compliance Costs: A Festschrift for Cedric Sandford* (Prospect Media): 273–95.

Sandford, Cedric (1989). General Report Administrative and Compliance Costs of Taxation. *Cahiers de Droit Fiscal International* 74b: 19–40.

Sandford, Cedric, ed. (1995). *Tax Compliance Costs: Measurement and Policy*. Fiscal Publications.

Sandford, Cedric, Michael Godwin, and Peter Hardwick (1989). *Administrative and Compliance Costs of Taxation*. Fiscal Publications.

Sandford, Cedric, and John Hasseldine (1992). *The Compliance Costs of Business Taxes in New Zealand*. Institute of Policy Studies.

Sandmo, Agnar (1976). Optimal Taxation – An Introduction to the Literature. *Journal of Public Economics* 6, 1-2: 37–54.

Slemrod, Joel (1990). Optimal Taxation and Optimal Tax Systems. *Journal of Economic Perspectives* 4, 1: 157–78.

Slemrod, Joel (2004). Written Testimony Submitted to the Committee on Ways and Means. Subcommittee on Oversight. Hearing on Tax Simplification (June 15).

Slemrod, Joel, and Marsha Blumenthal (1996). The Income Tax Compliance Cost of Big Business. *Public Finance Quarterly* 24, 4: 411–38.

Slemrod, Joel, and Varsha Venkatesh (2002). *The Income Tax Compliance Cost of Large and Mid-Size Business*. Report to the IRS LMSB Division. Internal Revenue Service.

Statistics Canada (2006a). *Canadian Labour Market at a Glance 2005*. Catalogue no. 71-222-XIE. Statistics Canada.

Statistics Canada (2006b). Social Simulation Database and Model (SPSD/M), Version 14.1. Catalogue No. 89F0002XCB. Statistics Canada, Socio-Economic Analysis and Modeling Division.

Statistics Canada (2006c). *Survey of Employment, Payrolls and Hours (SEPH)* (March). Statistics Canada.

Statistics Canada, Income and Expenditure Accounts Division (2006). *System of National Accounts: Provincial Economic Accounts*.

Tran-Nam, Binh (2001). Tax Compliance Costs Methodology – A Research Agenda for the Future Research. In C. Evans, J. Pope and J. Hasseldine, eds., *Taxation Compliance Costs: A Festschrift for Cedric Sandford* (Prospect Media): 51–68

United States Government Accountability Office [US GAO] (2005). *Tax Policy: Summary of Estimates of the Costs of the Federal Tax System*. US GAO.

Vaillancourt, François (1987). The Compliance Costs of Taxes on Business and Individuals: A Review of the Evidence. *Public Finance* 42, 3: 395–414.

Vaillancourt, François (1989). *The Administrative and Compliance Costs of the Personal Income Tax and Payroll Tax System in Canada, 1986*. Canadian Tax Paper 86. Canadian Tax Foundation.

Vaillancourt, François (1993). *The Compliance Costs of Sales Taxes in Canada: Evidence from the Eighties, Prospects for the Nineties*. Symposium on the Simplification of the Federal/Provincial Sales Tax System. Canadian Tax Foundation.

Vaillancourt, François (1999). Les coûts de conformité à la fiscalité des firmes et des individus : une recension des écrits. *L'Actualité économique* 75, 1-2-3 (March-June-September): 215–37.

Vaillancourt, François, and Etienne Blais (1995). The Evolution of Compliance Time of Personal Income Tax-filers in Canada 1971-1993. In Cedric Sandford, ed., *Tax Compliance Costs: Measurement and Policy* (Fiscal Publications): 263–72.

Veldhuis, Niels (2006). Presentation to the British Columbia Provincial Sales Taxes Review Panel (January 19, 2006). The Fraser Institute. Available upon request.

Wallschutzky, Ian (1994). Cost of Compliance for Small Business: Results from Twelve Case Studies in Australia. In Cedric Sandford, ed., *Tax Compliance Costs: Measurement and Policy* (Fiscal Publications): 275-298.

Wurts, Brian (1995). Report on the Plamondon Compliance Cost Study for the Canadian Goods and Services Tax. In Cedric Sandford, ed., *Tax Compliance Costs: Measurement and Policy* (Fiscal Publications): 299–320.

Chapter 4

Lessons from Abroad— Flat Tax in Practice

Patrick Basham and Daniel Mitchell

The North American discussion of the flat tax could be characterized as "nice theory, but not practical." Some doubters think a flat tax would not work if it were implemented. Others think that ideological objections are too formidable or that beneficiaries of current tax preferences are too powerful to overcome, meaning a flat tax will never get enacted.

In truth, the flat tax is anything but a policy experiment. There are now more than 20 jurisdictions using the flat tax and this number is expected to continue growing. Most of the flat-tax nations are transition economies in Eastern and Central Europe but there are a handful of wealthy economies that use this simple and fair tax system. In other words, the flat tax is a proven instrument of sound fiscal policy. The international evidence, combined with traditional research on tax policy, shows clearly that Canada would benefit greatly from adopting the flat tax.

The modern flat tax has a record of accomplishment that is six decades long. The Southeast Asian territory of Hong Kong built itself into an economic giant upon the fiscal anchor of the flat tax, a system that has been so successful that it survived the jurisdiction's transition from a British colony to a special administrative region of China (Littlewood, 2007). It is almost a half-century since the island of Guernsey, a British territory located in the English Channel off the northwest coast of France, joined its Channel Island neighbor, Jersey, as a flat-tax jurisdiction. More recently, a number of central and eastern European countries have enacted flat taxes on personal or corporate income, or both.[1]

This account of the international experience with the flat tax pays particular attention to the Central and Eastern European region for several reasons. First, these countries are the most recent converts to the flat tax as a cornerstone of fiscal policy. Therefore, they provide a contemporaneous illustration of the economic advantages that generally accompany adoption of the flat tax. Second, the fact that a majority of these formerly Communist nations, most notably Russia, has chosen to ditch the "progressive" tax system (that is, the higher one's income level, the higher one's tax rate) in favor of a flat-tax system speaks volumes about the desirability of a tax system so clearly antithetical to the ideological values propagated throughout Soviet-controlled Central and Eastern Europe between the end of World War II and the fall of the Berlin Wall.

Third, an analysis of the comparative ease with which these Eastern European countries have instituted their flat taxes reveals, upon closer inspection, the degree to which politics matters. That is, the idea of a flat tax is no more or less relevant to Central and Eastern European economies than it is to the Canadian economy. Nevertheless, almost without exception the political sponsors of flat taxes in Central and Eastern Europe faced limited institutional opposition that paled in comparison with the myriad of extremely powerful, vested interests in Canada that to date have limited the prospects for the discussion, promotion, and eventual passage of a Canadian flat tax.

Finally, globalization is leading to greater tax competition among nations and this means that the list of flat-tax nations is likely to grow. It is now increasingly easy for jobs and capital to cross national borders, and policy-makers face growing pressure to reform tax system in the contest to attract jobs and investment.

---

1 ◆ These countries feature single-rate tax systems, though they sometimes deviate substantially from the integrated flat-tax system favored by economists, which is based on both a single rate and a consumption base (meaning no double taxation of income that is saved and invested).

The flat tax in practice

Economist Andrei Grecu explained how Canadian policy-makers might learn from the experience of those countries that have adopted the flat tax:

> Analysing the economy of countries in which the flat tax is in place is a good start for assessing the potential of the flat tax to replace a progressive tax system. Of course, every country is a unique case, and the tax system is only one of the numerous factors influencing an economy. But looking at economic developments in a series of countries that have gone through the same kind of fiscal reforms will show the possible advantages of implementing the flat tax. (Grecu, 2004: 12)

The flat tax is certainly not a new fiscal policy instrument. When income taxes were first implemented, during the first half of the nineteenth century, many industrializing European nations chose flat rate systems.[2] Interestingly, flat-tax regimes were seen as a way of ensuring fairness. Prior to the flat tax's introduction, some nobles and clergymen escaped the payment of income tax entirely, as in eighteenth-century pre-revolutionary France. A principal attraction of the flat tax, therefore, was it ensured the nobility and the clergy paid their fair share of tax.

During the nineteenth century, however, many European nations experienced the spreading ideological influence of Karl Marx, the coauthor of the *Communist Manifesto* and proselytizer of revolutionary, left-wing economics. For Marx, the implementation of "a heavy progressive or graduated income tax" (Engels and Marx, 1848) was a priority item on the path to a classless communist society. As democratic politics gradually moved to the ideological Left during the second half of the nineteenth century, most European nations introduced

---

2 ◆ The first US income tax, enacted in 1861 to help finance the Civil War, had a flat rate of 3%, though graduated rates were imposed the following year. For more information, see Tax History Museum (1997–2006).

progressive tax systems featuring several rates to ensure that those earning a higher income paid the most tax (Adams, 2001).

In addition to its historical antecedents, the flat tax has strong theoretical underpinnings, as explained elsewhere in this book. Today, there is an impressive and growing subfield of economic research on the flat tax, itself.[3] There is also a large literature identifying the strongly negative relationship between high taxes and economic growth.[4] Fundamental tax reform addresses this problem. Alvin Rabushka and Robert Hall explain that a flat tax will mean that

> [i]mproved incentives to work through increased take-home wages will stimulate work effort and raise total output. Rational investment incentives will raise the overall level of investment and channel it into the most productive areas. And sharply lower taxes on entrepreneurial effort will enhance this critical input to the economy. (Hall and Rabushka, 2007: 127)

This is in stark contrast to the current system. Grecu argued that the progressive "income tax is not only complex, it is perverse, diverting energy and resources into uneconomic behaviour forced upon people by the tax code itself." He maintained that, "[i]n terms of growth foregone and effort misplaced, its [the progressive tax system's] economic costs reach into billions of pounds each year, maybe tens of billions" (*EurActiv.com*, 2006, November 9).

Under a pure flat tax, the tax man takes the same cut from the last dollar of taxable income you earn as he took from the first.[5] Proponents contend that the introduction of a flat tax minimizes the disincentive to work more and earn more (as well as to save and invest more) that exists under a graduated, progressive tax system. Hence, a simplified tax system featuring a low, flat rate will lead to more efficient economic decision-making.

---

3 ◆ See the review of the flat tax literature in Clemens et al., 2003.

4 ◆ See, for example, the research literature review provided in Leach, 2003.

5 ◆ In practice, most flat-tax systems contain generous personal exemptions. Therefore, the tax on your first dollar earned is not equal to the tax on your last dollar earned.

While the evidence discussed throughout this chapter informs us that the flat tax is a sound and sensible policy, it is not a panacea. Economic success is also dependent upon such factors as the regulatory climate, as well as monetary and trade policies. However, the international evidence strongly suggests that the flat tax is a significant contributor to fast-paced economic growth.

More than 20 jurisdictions now have flat-tax systems and all but three of those countries have enacted the flat tax since 1994 (table 4.1). A quarter of all European countries employ a flat tax on either personal or corporate income or both, and these countries provide a global, or at least a regional, proving ground for the flat-tax concept.[6]

In North American policy-making circles, where a national flat tax is characterized as a fine theoretical idea without practical application, the discussion is largely uninformed. The flat tax not only has a long-standing, tangible history but, in practice, is working as well as its proponents predicted it would. As Matthew Lynn, a European business journalist, observed:

> Economists can debate the [flat tax] theory endlessly ... Yet this debate doesn't have to be conducted in charts, or tested only in lecture halls. Flat taxes have been introduced in several former communist countries ... In different countries, flat taxes would produce varied outcomes. Still, there is no escaping the evidence. Where they have been introduced, flat taxes are yielding impressive results. (Lynn 2004)

Pessimistic predictions about the flat tax have been proven wrong.[7] The flat tax has stimulated positive economic news across the board, including improved economic growth rates.[8] The *Economist* magazine found that, "Flat taxes have stoked prosperity in every country that has

---

6 ◆ See, for example, the discussion in Tzortzis, 2005.

7 ◆ See, for example, the discussion in Aligica and Terpe, 2005.

8 ◆ Simeonova, 2007. See, also *Wall Street Journal*, 2007, April 17. For an earlier discussion of the flat tax's potential to increase economic growth rates, see Stokey and Rebelo, 1995; Ventura, 1999.

Table 4.1: Flat-tax jurisdictions—personal income taxes

Jurisdiction	Year of enactment	Tax rate
Jersey	1940	20%
Hong Kong	1947	16%
Guernsey	1960	20%
Jamaica	1986	25% (orig. 33%)
Estonia	1994	21% (orig. 26%)
Latvia	1995	25%
Lithuania	1996	24% (orig. 33%)
Russia	2001	13%
Serbia	2003	14%
Iraq	2004	15%
Slovakia	2004	19%
Ukraine	2004	15% (orig. 13%)
Georgia	2005	12%
Romania	2005	16%
Albania	2007	10%
Iceland	2007	35.70%
Krgyzstan	2007	10%
Macedonia	2007	10%
Mongolia	2007	10%
Montenegro	2007	15%
Bulgaria	2008	10%
Czech Republic	2008	15%
Mauritius	2009	15%

Source: Mitchell, 2007c: 10.

adopted them" (*Economist*, 2006, June 1). In 2004, for example, GDP growth rates in those countries with a flat tax exceeded the worldwide, average, growth rate of major industrialized countries (*Wall Street Journal*, 2005, October 7). Transition economies should grow faster, of course, as part of a convergence process but transition economies with flat-tax systems are growing more rapidly than transition economies with so-called progressive tax rates.

According to the Economist Intelligence Unit, flat-tax rates are unlikely to undermine government revenue (Economist Intelligence Unit, 2005). In fact, revenue did not dry up in those countries that adopted the flat tax. This revenue outcome comes as a surprise to many, although it should not, as there exists a strong correlation between low or reduced tax levels and revenue stability. Most recently, for example, a KPMG International study of 86 countries found that those countries that cut corporate taxes both attracted business investment and maintained previous revenue levels (Kennedy, 2007).

The "experts" deployed by multinational organizations have been proven incorrect in their advice and forecasts regarding the flat tax. The Cato Institute's Daniel J. Mitchell, an expert on the flat tax, recalls that, in the case of Central and Eastern Europe, "the International Monetary Fund played no positive role in ... successful economic reforms. Indeed, in many former Soviet Bloc nations, the IMF has created roadblocks to tax reform, and often has urged governments to raise taxes instead" (Mitchell, 2003b).

It should come as no surprise that the former communist countries of Central and Eastern Europe were the first to experiment with the flat tax. After all, most of them in effect were starting with a blank fiscal slate. Immediately after breaking free from communism, most of them imported the kind of discriminatory tax structure found in Western Europe but policy makers concluded (and are still concluding) that graduated rate structures discourage economic activity. Consequently, they opted for the simplest, most efficient system.[9]

The Baltics took the lead, with Estonia becoming the first of the post-communist nations to adopt the flat tax. Lithuania and Latvia

---

9 ◆ See, for example, the discussion in Henninger, 2006.

quickly followed. Since their adoption of a flat tax, the three Baltic nations have experienced such strong economic growth, increases in foreign investment, and declines in unemployment that they are now known as the "Baltic Tigers."

As seen in table 1, other nations are playing follow the leader, with good results. According to Philip Poole, head of research into emerging markets at HSBC in London, a lower, flatter corporate tax has been "an important part of the story in strengthening growth, balances of payments, fiscal performance and currencies" in Eastern Europe (Kennedy, 2007: 5). Hence, as economist Alvin Rabushka observed, "the flat tax has become an integral part of the fiscal landscape in Central and Eastern Europe, from Estonia in the North, to Russia in the East, Georgia in the South, and Slovakia in the West" (Rabushka, 2005c).

The flat tax portends the end of special-interest tax breaks and favors, as a flat tax system is largely or completely free of deductions, exemptions, and exceptions, thereby eliminating the complex rules and loopholes that characterize progressive tax systems. The flat tax constitutes a clean tax system once most preferential treatment is abolished (Berggren, 2003). Consequently, both the declaration of taxes and tax transparency are heightened. The international experience with the flat tax demonstrates that tax evasion is reduced as activity is shifted from the black to the legitimate economy.[10]

As flat tax rates are relatively low, the incentive for tax evasion is also reduced, usually by a significant margin. The Adam Smith Institute's Madsen Pirie noted that, "The point of the flat tax is that it broadens the tax base. People avoid less, evade less and declare more" (Pirie, 2005). Pirie found that if a government has, "set the [flat tax] rate low enough … it just isn't worth going criminal" (Underhill, 2007). Mitchell also found that the flat tax "has curtailed interest-group pleading in Eastern Europe" (Mitchell, 2005).

When it comes to the serious problems of corruption, inconsistent implementation of laws, high volumes of unregistered trade, and low protection of property rights, Natasha Srdoc-Samy, president of Croatia's Adriatic Institute for Public Policy, found that, "Flat taxes

---

10 ◆ See the discussion in Herbert, 2005.

help counteract such problems by closing loopholes and unmasking evasion techniques." She summarized the post-communist Central and Eastern European experience thus: "Flat taxes also carry a promise to free up economies for growth, by forcing gray economic activity into the legitimate market and simplifying collection. Economic activity increases, and so does honest reporting of income, while tax evasion drops" (Srdoc-Samy, 2007).

Although the absence of a withholding tax in Hong Kong constitutes a significant difference between the Hong Kong and European versions, the flat tax is simple to understand and simple to pay in both Europe and Hong Kong. The straightforwardness of the flat tax system vastly reduces the cost to the tax collector. Even more important, taxpayers are much less likely to need professional assistance to comply with a simple tax code, which is another reason why the flat tax saves taxpayers enormous sums of money. Billions of dollars are saved in compliance costs, as a tax return can be filled in quickly with a minimum of paperwork (Herbert, 2005).

Hong Kong

Hong Kong has had a flat-tax system since the Inland Revenue Ordinance of 1947.[11] Individuals can choose to pay a 16% flat tax (15% beginning in 2008). Alternatively, they can choose to pay tax based on a system with four graduated rates (2%, 8%, 12%, and 17%) and various deductions. Because this alternative system has a generous allowance, the majority of taxpayers among Hong Kong's 6.9 million residents do not even have to worry about selecting the flat-tax option.

Sixty years later, Hong Kong remains the administrator of arguably the world's most efficient tax system (Edwards, 2005a). Consider that the American federal income tax generates 66,000 pages of code and regulations. In practice, highly complicated returns can require an American taxpayer to fill out dozens of separate forms. Indeed, the IRS "forms and publications" web site actually gives taxpayers 1,036 options (Internal Revenue Service, 2007). Unsurprisingly, 60%

---

11 ◆ For additional economic and historical analyses of Hong Kong's flat tax, see Reynolds, 1999 and Rabushka, 1979. See also Emes et al., 2001.

of American taxpayers require professional help to complete their tax returns (Moore, 2007). By comparison, Hong Kong's entire tax code is no more than 200 pages (Kerr, 2007). Grecu found that "[t]his combination of simplicity and low level of taxation has reduced the adverse effects of taxation on work effort, saving, and risk-taking and was a key factor in Hong's remarkable economic growth and development" (Grecu, 2004: 13).

Hong Kong has been the world's fastest growing economy over the past 50 years (Mitchell, 2003a). Between 1950 and 1981, Hong Kong ran a fiscal surplus in 27 of those years (Grecu, 2004: 13). Far more impressive, however, is that Hong Kong has constrained the burden of government. Budgetary outlays currently consume only 16% of GDP and government policy is not to allow spending too climb beyond 20% of GDP. Compared to other industrialized nations, where governments consume about 40% of GDP, that's an especially impressive statistic.

No wonder Hong Kong is the world's freest economy (Gwartney et al., 2006: 97). According to the *Economist*, "The territory's tradition of simple and low taxes ... is widely seen as a main reason for its stunning rise to prosperity" (*Economist*, 2000, February 24). Its unparalleled success is indeed based upon a non-interventionist economy policy centred on its income tax system and supplemented by the absence of a pension-related payroll, general sales, or value added tax, and the lack of tariffs on imported goods (Grecu, 2004: 12–13). In 2006, government spending constituted only 17% of GDP compared with an OECD average of over 40% (Long, 2007: 10). Economist Alan Reynolds, a tax specialist and an expert on Hong Kong's fiscal experience, pointed out that "[t]he Hong Kong tax system has one major advantage over even the most elegant theoretical alternatives. It has been tested for more than 50 years. It works" (Reynolds, 2005).

During the past decade, the Hong Kong economy had to withstand Asia's 1997 financial crisis, the bursting of America's dot-com bubble, and the bird-flu and SARS epidemics. Yet, Hong Kong's tax system continues to provide a fiscal environment within which the economy can flourish. Since 1997, the number of multinational companies with regional headquarters in Hong Kong has increased by one third. There also have been billions in capital raised through hundreds of initial public offerings (Kleinman, 2007). Between 2004 and 2006, Hong Kong's economy grew at its highest rate for two decades, with economic growth of 7.5% in 2005 and 6.9% in 2006. In 2006, GDP per capita stood at an impressive US$37,300 (Long, 2007: 4, 9).

Channel Islands

The British Crown bestows upon the Channel Islands of Guernsey and Jersey a special constitutional status, which grants them autonomy over fiscal policy. Both Guernsey and Jersey have had flat taxes on personal incomes for several decades.[12] Jersey was the first to introduce a flat tax: in 1940 the island switched from the British income-tax code to a 20% flat tax on both individual and corporate income. Guernsey followed Jersey's fiscal policy example in 1960.

Grecu contended that "[t]he Channel Islands offer an even more convincing example of flat tax efficiency" (Grecu, 2004: 12) than does Hong Kong. Grecu found that "[e]conomic performance in the Channel Islands proves once again that the efficiency, simplicity, and fairness induced by a flat tax have a positive influence upon economic growth, employment, and the overall standard of living" (Grecu, 2004: 13). To be sure, the Channel Islands also are rich in part because they serve as offshore financial centers, meaning that they benefit not only from their wise decisions about taxation but also from the misguided decisions of nations with oppressive tax regimes.

Since Jersey and Guernsey introduced the flat tax, their economies have grown far more quickly than the British economy (Grecu, 2004: 12). For 67 years, in the case of Jersey, and for 47 years, in Guernsey's case, the economy has performed extremely, and consistently, well. Jersey's GDP, for example, grew 90% in real terms between 1980 and 1990. Meanwhile, Guernsey's GDP has more than tripled since the introduction of a flat tax. Income-tax receipts account for 90% of Jersey government revenue, while 74% of the revenue received by the Guernsey government comes from income-tax receipts (Grecu, 2004: 13).

The flat tax is a major contributor to the wealth enjoyed by these British Crown dependencies (Mitchell, 2005). The research conducted

---

12 ◆ See the discussion in Emes et al., 2001: 54–55.

by Grecu found that "[a] combination of low taxation, stable government, and lack of party politics has brought huge wealth to the Channel Islands by maintaining a highly attractive business environment" (Grecu, 2004: 13). Nevertheless, Guernsey has not rested on the laurels of a 20% flat tax on corporate and personal incomes. In July 2006, the Guernsey legislature approved a zero corporate tax rate and capped the maximum tax on individuals at £250,000 (CDN$530,000) (Hall and Rabushka, 2007: 11).

Central and Eastern Europe

Although both jurisdictions have autonomy over fiscal issues, neither Hong Kong nor the Channel Islands are independent or autonomous countries. Therefore, the next section describes and analyzes the flat tax experience to date in Central and Eastern Europe. The flat tax reforms implemented throughout Central and Eastern Europe vary in the degree of comprehensiveness, as the following analyses show.[13] Estonia was the first European nation to adopt the flat tax. Russia is the most important economy to have adopted the flat tax. As the most developed European economy with a flat tax, Slovakia may be the best comparison for Canadian policy-makers. As of 2007, Lithuania, Lativa, Serbia, the Ukraine, Georgia, Romania, Macedonia, Montenegro, and Albania had also adopted a flat tax. The Czech Republic and Bulgaria will do so in 2008.

Estonia

When Prime Minister Mart Laar's government took office in 1992, inflation in newly post-Soviet Estonia was running at an annual rate of over 1,000%, the economy had shrunk 30% in two years, and unemployment topped 30%. The economic situation was so dire that food was rationed and cars were not seen on the streets for lack of gasoline (*Mongabay. com*, 1986–1998). Laar concluded that radical economy surgery was required. The next year, his government passed flat-tax legislation. On January 1, 1994, against the International Monetary Fund's advice (*Slate*,

---

13 ◆ See the discussion in Heath, 2006: ch. 6. See, too, Grabowski and Tomalak, 2004 for a detailed review of the economic reforms implemented throughout the region.

2005), Estonia became the first European country to implement a flat tax. Three tax rates on personal income and one on corporate profits were replaced with one uniform rate of 26%. The only remaining exemptions apply to those living on government pensions and those with three or more children. A study by the British government of the Estonian experience found "no transitional problems in moving to the flat rate, instead it helped to solve existing problems such as the high inflation rate which led to changing levels of income for each tax bracket."[14]

With hindsight, it is clear that, as the *Economist* observed, "[a]t the stroke of a pen, this tiny Baltic nation transformed itself from backwater to bellwether" (*Economist*, 2005, April 14a). Within a year of the flat tax's introduction, unemployment had fallen to 6%. A decade later, Estonians enjoyed low inflation and low unemployment, and the Estonian government's budget has been in surplus since 2001 (Hall and Rabushka, 2007: 8). The flat tax led to higher productivity levels and, consequently, higher wages (Grecu, 2004: 14). The country is on course to double living standards every six years (*Economist*, 2006, December 13).

Estonia's flat-tax rate was cut by two percentage points to 24% in 2005, by a further two percentage points to 22% in 2006, and reduced to 20% in 2007. It is scheduled to fall to 18% by 2009 (Heath, 2006: 83). Estonia can afford to keep cutting its tax rate because its economy is booming and this is generating a lot of additional tax revenue. Indeed, personal income-tax revenues have nearly doubled since 2000 and corporate tax receipts have jumped by more than 300% (Mitchell, 2007a). The rate could be dropped even faster if lawmakers chose not to use so much of the new revenue to finance additional government spending.

But, even if spending is climbing too rapidly, it is hard to argue with success. The country has experienced impressive rates of economic growth. Estonia has averaged real, annual, economic growth of 5.7% since 1995 (Edwards, 2005a). Real GDP growth this year is forecast at more than 8% (Hansen, 2006). As a result, revenue continues to pour into the government's coffers. Critics had predicted that repealing its

---

14 ◆ Study published by the UK Government Treasury Department; reported in Trefgarne, 2005.

high tax rates on wealthy citizens would erode the country's tax base. This did not happen. In 1993, government revenues were 39.4% of GDP; in 2002, they were 39.6% (*Economist*, 2005, April 14a). According to the Bank of Estonia, government revenue rose by one third between 2001 and 2003 (Lynn, 2004). The government's budget is balanced and the country has no net foreign debt (*Economist*, 2006, December 13).

In practice, the corporate income tax has been abolished. Estonian companies withhold and pay tax on the dividends they send to shareholders and they also pay tax on the fringe benefits they supply to workers, but there is no tax on earnings (Mitchell, 2007a). This means no double taxation on corporate income. Estonia is now a magnet for financial and human capital. For example, foreign direct investment has more than quadrupled, according to the United Nations Conference on Trade and Development's Foreign Direct Investment Database (Heath, 2006: 88). In fact, Estonia is now Europe's biggest per-capita recipient of foreign investment (*Economist*, 2006, December 13).

The simplified tax system means that 80% of Estonians spend only a few minutes online filing an annual tax return (*Economist*, 2005, October 13). Unsurprisingly, then, among Estonians the flat tax is now an article of faith (Landler, 2005).

Russia

The success of Estonia's experiment with the flat tax encouraged a radical reform of the Russian tax code, a reform launched in 1998 with the goal of reducing the tax burden on individuals and corporations. On January 1, 2001, Russia collapsed its three personal income-tax rates of 12%, 20%, and 30% into a flat 13% tax on all personal income.[15] There are also deductions for charitable contributions, as well as deductions for educational and medical expenses. The corporate tax rate was reduced from 35% to 24%.[16]

---

15 ◆ Rabushka, 2004; for a recent overview of the reform process, see Konnovm, 2007.

16 ◆ In stark contrast, companies based in the United States still pay a 35% tax, which is the second-highest corporate tax among industrialized nations. See Mitchell, 2003a.

In *Flat Tax: Towards a British Model*, Allister Heath concluded that "[t]he flat tax has been a key reason—in addition to soaring commodity prices—why the Russian economy has grown strongly" (Heath, 2006: 82–83). The Russian economy has indeed grown rapidly since the introduction of a flat tax almost seven years ago. In 2001, the first year of the flat tax, the country's real GDP rose by 5.1%. GDP rose a further 4.7% in 2002 and a massive 7.3% in 2003. Since reforming its tax system, Russia has demonstrated that it has the potential to join the ranks of the world's leading economic powers (Beschloss, 2007). Economic growth has averaged over 6% annually since the flat tax was introduced, an economic growth rate that far out-paces that of the American or European Union economies (Beschloss, 2007). All of which has produced rising disposable incomes among the Russian people themselves (Koza, 2007).

Russia has recorded a remarkable turnaround in government revenues. Receipts from income tax have grown faster than overall revenues and other taxes (Rabushka, 2005b). Revenues rose by more than 20% in each of the flat tax's first two years (Evans, 2007: 8–9). After one year, the new flat tax on personal income had raised 25.2% more revenue in real terms than its progressive predecessor (Rabushka, 2004; *Economist*, 2005, April 14a; *Boston Globe*, 2005). The following year, personal income-tax revenue rose 24.6% in real terms (Rabushka, 2004). In 2003, personal income tax revenue rose a further 15.2% in real terms (Rabushka, 2004). After adjusting for inflation, personal income-tax revenue rose an additional 16% in 2004 (Lynn, 2004). That meant total real receipts from the personal income tax more than doubled four years after the implementation of the flat tax (Hall and Rabushka, 2007: 8). Heath commented:

> Unsurprisingly, some politicians and international bodies (and notably the IMF) (Ivanova et al., 2005) have claimed that this surge in revenues had little to do with the flat tax and all to do with a crackdown on tax evasion. They are right to question whether all the revenue increase came from the flat tax—it didn't, of course, but nobody is claiming that. (Heath, 2006: 83).

According to Grecu, "[t]his constant expansion of the government tax revenue is the result of less tax evasion and increased incentives to work, save, and invest" (Lynn, 2004). Russia has practically repaid its IMF debt and now holds foreign currency reserves that exceed CAD$260 billion (Beschloss, 2007).

Compliance by taxpayers has improved dramatically (Rabushka, 2004). In 2000, for example, Russians in the two higher tax brackets reported only 52% of their income to the government. During the first year of the flat tax, these same taxpayers reported 68% of their income (Ivanova et al., 2005).

Slovakia

The Baltic nations started the tax-reform process in Eastern Europe. Russia's reforms made the flat tax more visible. So, it was just a matter of time before the idea spread and one of the most impressive stories is Slovakia. Heath characterized Slovakia as "[a] case study of a post-communist, transition economy successfully overhauling its economy" (Heath, 2006: 84).

After the Cold War ended, most Central and Eastern European countries, including Slovakia, modeled their new tax systems on the progressive tax systems in place in Western Europe and North America. Slovakia's progressive system featured five income brackets between 10% and 38%. It also featured 90 exemptions, 19 potential sources of untaxed income, 66 tax-exempt items, and 27 items with specific tax rates (Tzortzis, 2005; Butler, 2004).

In January 2004, Slovakia became the sixth Eastern European, and the first OECD, country to adopt a flat tax.[17] Slovakia's flat tax is very comprehensive, rivalling Estonia and Hong Kong for having the system closest to the theoretical ideal. Key features include a single 19% tax rate on personal income and corporate income, as well as a 19% value-added tax. This uniform 19% rate has been very successful, boosting growth and producing higher tax revenues for the government (*Economist*, 2005, March 3; Fund, 2005). A March 2005 report by the Dutch investment bank ING stated:

---

17 ◆ For more information, see Chren, 2006.

[T]he flat tax regime has seen a better-than-expected increase in tax collection. The government was surprised to see that the flat tax is a huge marketing tool for foreign corporate investors. Slovakia is now a prime example of a transparent and simple tax system with very low tax rates. Presently, the tax regime is an important factor supporting FDI inflow to the country next to low labour costs, low asset prices, EU membership, etc. (ING, 2005)

The new system has no exemptions and only two deductions, for pensions and charitable contributions. The new tax code's simplicity has led to greater transparency and a reduction in tax evasion (Tzortzis, 2005). According to researchers from the Harvard Business School, Slovakia "implemented one of the most simple, neutral, and effective systems in the world that improved the business environment, reduced tax evasion and, in connection with other reforms, brought about high and sustainable economic growth" (Lagace, 2007).

Slovakia is today the economic reform star of central Europe. The attractive combination of a flat tax, a deregulated labour market, and a well-run, funded pension system has resulted in a flood of foreign investment, which has stimulated economic growth (*Economist*, 2006, June 1; 2005, March 3). In 2004, the World Bank named Slovakia the world's top economic reformer. In the six years preceding the introduction of a flat tax, economic growth averaged 3.4%. Since the flat tax's introduction, Slovakian economic growth has been among the highest in Europe. In 2005, the Slovakian economy grew by 6%; growth in 2006 measured 8.3%, a record high. In 2007, GDP growth is forecast to reach 8.9% (*Dow Jones Newswire*, 2007).

Slovakia has benefited from the significant inflow of foreign investment, especially by automobile and electronics companies, such as Kia Motors, Peugeot, Volkswagen, and Samsung (*Dow Jones Newswire*, 2007). In 2005, total foreign direct investment was six times more than it was in 1998 (Heath, 2006: 93). In fact, the flood of foreign car companies into the country has caused Slovakia to be called the "Detroit of Europe" (Mitchell, 2006). According to corporate executive, Ivan Kocis, the flat tax is "a very important factor" (Tzortrzis, 2005) in attracting these new companies.

Other members of the "flat tax club"

Although Estonia, Russia, and Slovakia have received most of the attention and the lion's share of the plaudits, several other Central and Eastern European countries have very successfully adopted the flat tax. Lithuania introduced a flat-tax rate of 33% on personal income in 1994, which has been subsequently reduced to 27% (Heath, 2006: 89; also Rabushka, 2005a). The Lithuanian economy has been among the fastest growing in Europe. From 2002 to 2004, real GDP growth averaged an impressive 5.6% (Grecu, 2004: 14). Since the adoption of a flat tax, the decline of tax evasion and higher economic growth combined to increase tax revenues. Lithuanians also have seen declining unemployment and a rising standard of living. Lithuania's Baltic neighbour, Latvia, adopted a 25% flat tax in 1995. Latvia's real growth in GDP over the period from 2001 to 2004 also averaged 5.6% (Grecu, 2004: 14).

Borrowing directly from the Russian model, in 2003 Serbia introduced a 14% flat tax on salaries. Different flat rates are levied on alternative sources of income. Under the Serbian system, a personal allowance is set at 40% of the average wage and taxpayers are eligible for a further deduction worth 15% of the average annual salary per dependent. In 2004, the Ukraine introduced a flat tax of 13% (which now has climbed to 15%, an unfortunate change that was included in the original legislation). This replaced the old five-bracket, progressive system that had a top rate of 40%. January 2005 saw Georgia introduce a 12% flat tax. The flat tax replaced the former four-rate progressive system whose top rate had been 20%. The new tax structure reduced the size and weight of the country's previous tax code by 95% (Rabushka, 2005d).

At the same time, Romania's progressive tax system, which featured five personal tax brackets ranging between 18% and 40%, was replaced by a 16% flat tax on corporate and personal income. In only two years, the Romanian flat tax has been a tremendous success.[18] As Hall and Rabushka wrote, "Romania's Finance Ministry reported that income-tax revenue for the first eight months of 2006 greatly exceeded estimates and that the state budget had a significant surplus at the end of July" (Hall and Rabushka, 2007: 9). Revenue has continued to rise over the

---

18 ◆ See the discussion in Heath, 2006: 97–98.

past two years (Ionita, 2006; also BBC, 2007; Muntean, 2007). Romania has also experienced a remarkable decline in the underground economy (ROMPRES, 2007). During the flat tax's inaugural year, unemployment fell to 5.5% in 2005, a 13-year low (Heath, 2006: 97).

More recently, on January 1, 2007, Macedonia introduced a 12% flat tax on personal and corporate incomes. It replaced a progressive system that featured personal tax rates that ranged between 15% and 24% (Hall and Rabushka, 2007: 9). The government pledged to reduce the flat rate to 10% in 2008. Prime Minister Nikola Gruevski is confident that "[t]his reform will decrease tax evasion and encourage people to meet their obligations to the state" (Reynolds, 2007: B2).

On July 1, 2007, neighboring Montenegro instituted a flat tax of 15% on personal income. The rate will be lowered to 12% in 2008 and further lowered to 9% in 2009. In Albania, a 10% flat tax on corporate and personal incomes also came into effect on July 1, 2007. In April 2007, Czech Prime Minister Mirek Topolanek announced that the personal income-tax rate would fall to a flat 15% in 2008, replacing progressive rates of 12% to 32% (*Wall Street Journal*, 2007, April 17). The Bulgarians are the latest converts to a flat tax system. On July 29, 2007, the Bulgarian cabinet approved a 10% flat-tax rate. With subsequent approval from the parliament, the new tax rate will be effective January 1, 2008.

Taxation politics—why some countries choose to be flat

The economic argument for adoption of a flat tax is a very strong one, indeed. The introduction of a flat tax, to cite one advantage, increases economic efficiency by reducing the progressive character of the income-tax system and, thereby, removing penalties for being more productive. However, whether Canada actually adopts the flat tax will depend as much upon political as economic considerations. Therefore, a discussion of the political factors that have encouraged adoption in Central and Eastern Europe, for example, will be useful as a contribution to the domestic debate.

As political factors are a fundamental determinant of the tax system (Poterba, 1998), what are the political factors that may bear on the reform of fiscal policy? The subfield of economics known as "public choice" sheds the most light upon this topic.[19] According to public-choice theory, politicians are self-interested actors, that is, their overriding motivation is the securing of votes and campaign donations. Public-choice theory suggests that tax policy is determined by politicians seeking mutually beneficial relationships with special-interest organizations and specific groups of voters. The bottom line is that politicians support tax reform when the new system is likely to provide them with more votes and greater campaign contributions than the current system.[20]

Stanley Winer and Walter Hettich investigated the influence of political factors on the nature of tax systems in democratic countries (Winer and Hettich, 1998). They found that the self-interested policy-maker would equate the political cost per dollar of revenue raised from different policy instruments, rather than the economic-efficiency cost. Hence, departures from an economically efficient tax system result from politicians' rational political, rather than economic, calculations. Consequently, politicians and bureaucrats tend to act in narrow, self-interested, ways that harm the broad national interest. For example, Roy E. Cordato and Sheldon L. Richman explained that a democratic political system is biased toward expanding the size of government (Cordato and Richman, 1986). Hence, Randall Holcombe's conclusion that "[d]emocracy contains an inherent bias toward inefficiently large government" (Holcombe, 1998: 366). Furthermore, Buchanan and Tullock found that "[a]lmost any conceivable collective action will provide more benefits to some citizens than others, and almost

---

19 ◆ For a recent discussion of the application of public-choice theory to the debate over implementing a flat tax, see Atkinson, 2004.

20 ◆ See, most recently, Berggren, 2003. See also Brennan and Buchanan, 1980; DiLorenzo, 1985; Hettich and Winer, 1985; Hettich and Winer, 1988; McCaleb, 1985; Wagner, 1985; Buchanan, 1987; Lee and Tollison, 1988; McChesney, 1988; Spindler and Walker, 1988; van Velthoven and van Winden, 1991; de Vanssay and Spindler, 1994.

any conceivable distribution of a given cost sum will bear more heavily on some individuals and groups than on others" (Buchanan and Tullock, 1962: 291). The economic benefits of government intervention are concentrated on smaller, well-organized groups while the costs are imposed on a larger, unorganized group. As Chris Edwards, a tax expert at the Cato Institute, summarized, "[l]egislators have a bias toward dishing out government largesse to visible and important constituencies, while hiding the resulting costs from current taxpayers" (Edwards, 2005b: 9).

Consequently, different tax systems are associated with different opportunities for seeking political rents (that is, benefits) (Poterba, 1998: 391). Economist James M. Poterba explained how and why specific tax policies are adopted. Poterba is in "no doubt that political factors, notably the political power of various interest groups, play a key role in the determination of tax policy ... tax policy is largely about equating the marginal political costs of different taxes" (Poterba, 1998: 395). Edwards, too, noted that, "Politicians will always be tempted to carve out narrow tax breaks for favored groups" (Edwards, 2005b: 5). The current Canadian tax code, therefore, reflects a gargantuan political balance that has determined the allocation of benefits to various special-interest groups. In short, political bargains were reached with particularly powerful Canadian interest groups, such as elderly voters (Poterba, 1998: 393).

Under such a preferential tax code, government encourages investment in activities that it deems to be in the public interest through deductions and credits. And although it is theoretically possible for a so-called progressive tax system to be free of loopholes, the very existence of higher tax rates generates the political pressure for special preferences. It is not surprising, therefore, that tax systems with graduated rates also contain a multiplicity of exemptions that distort taxpayers' behavior. Hence, as Richard Epstein stated, "[d]ecisions by citizens about where to set up their homes and businesses are not independent of the tax system" (Epstein, 2004: 14). Edwards explained that "[u]nder the current [progressive] tax system, with its multiple rates, deductions, and credits, politicians can use a divide-and-conquer strategy to confuse the public about who is affected by proposed cuts or increases"

(Edwards, 2005b: 15). This is especially relevant given that narrow tax provisions have potentially large effects on a small set of economic agents (Poterba, 1998: 392).

Anachronistic conceptions of fairness and social justice are the principal reason that Canada and most other Western countries have progressive tax systems. Public finance experts use the term "horizontal equity" to describe a system whereby individuals with similar incomes pay similar amounts of tax. However, Epstein reminded us that "[g]iven the vagaries of the political process, it cannot be assumed that the benefits of a public good are evenly spread across all individuals subject to taxation" (Epstein, 2004: 10). The progressive tax code's many exemptions, deductions, and credits ensure that, in practice, individuals are treated very unequally (Edwards, 2005b: 14).

Equality of treatment under the law is a cornerstone of the pure flat tax, as all taxpayers pay the same rate on their taxable income. Advocates of the flat tax appreciate that true equality places emphasis upon the economic starting, rather than finishing, line. Under a pure flat tax, there is no preferential tax treatment. The tax does not bestow an advantage upon any particular industry, or type of household, or specific business. When Illarionov advised President Putin on the flat tax, he explained that the flat tax signals "the neutrality of government tax policy towards different types of businesses, towards different types of industries and different types of income received in different sectors. Therefore, it ... leads to a much more efficient allocation of resources in the economy" (Frontier Centre for Public Policy, 2000).

Over the past several years, much of Central and Eastern Europe has simplified and flattened its tax structure. In striking contrast, Canada's clogged tax code is so laden with breaks, deductions, and exceptions that it retains nothing of its original shape.[21] Taxpayers must contend with more tax forms, longer tax instructions, and returns filled with more credits and deductions.

Canada's inefficient and costly progressive tax system survives largely (perhaps, entirely) because vested interests are willing to keep it complicated (Moore, 2007). Kevin Waddell, vice president of the

---

21 ◆ See, for example, Canada, Department of Finance, 2006.

Boston Consulting Group, articulated the obstacles to adopting the flat tax in Western European nations, obstacles that are equally apparent in the Canadian context. In Waddell's view, "[t]he challenge that Western Europe has is that you have a lot of entrenched interest groups. When you try and put in place a flat tax, you take something away from somebody else" (Tzortzis, 2005). Is the introduction of a flat tax in Canada, then, a lost cause? No, it is not a lost cause; or, rather, it need not be one. Canadian proponents of the flat tax can derive encouragement from the finding that a tax system cluttered with credits, deductions, and exemptions contains the seeds of its own destruction. As T.J. DiLorenzo explained:

> The granting of loopholes by politicians is subject to diminishing returns, just as all other activities are. The political benefit of granting additional tax preferences will fall over time. It is also likely that the political costs (to the politician) are rising, for with increased complexity of the tax system comes greater dissatisfaction on the part of voters who complain that the tax system is too complicated and unfair. Thus, at some point it is not politically profitable to create further loopholes. (DiLorenzo, 1985)

Furthermore, the *Economist* surmised that "[t]he more complicated a country's tax system becomes, the easier it is for governments to make it more complicated still, in an accelerating process of proliferating insanity—until, perhaps, a limit of madness is reached and a spasm of radical simplification is demanded" (*Economist*, 2005, April 14b). One trusts that the *Economist* is prescient and a "spasm of radical simplification" is imminent in Canada.

Proponents of the flat tax should be aware, however, that this process might prove to be cyclical (Spindler and Walker, 1988: 72; Buchanan, 1987: 33–34). DiLorenzo maintained that "once the slate is wiped clean and most loopholes are eliminated, the same politicians who benefited from voting for some version of the flat tax can then benefit further by 'starting over' and granting more loopholes, the marginal political value of which would then be relatively high" (DiLorenzo, 1985: 404). One must also bear in mind the cautionary tale offered by economists Xavier de Vanssay and Zane Spindler that rent-seeking competition over tax reform may diminish prospective efficiency gains (de Vanssay and Spindler, 1994).

How does flat tax reform succeed?

The experiences of Central and Eastern European countries with the flat tax is a contemporary example of how radical tax reform can succeed (see Evans, 2007). What are the political and economic conditions that have resulted in successful implementation of a flat-tax policy in this region? Politically successful flat-tax proposals in Central and Eastern Europe shared the following five characteristics.

1 ◆ It is easier to implement simpler, more radical reform than more complicated, piecemeal reform. Slow and partial reforms do not work; fast and deep ones do work. (*Economist*, 2006, June 1)

2 ◆ The rate of a flat tax needs to be set at a comparatively low level.

3 ◆ The lower the ratios of tax to GDP and government spending to GDP, the better.

4 ◆ Though there may be a tipping point of complexity that leads to the "spasm of radical simplification," the greater the number of current tax loopholes, the harder it is politically to introduce a flat tax, due to the entrenched resistance to change of special-interest groups. (Heath, 2006: 100–01)

5 ◆ Tax systems are often closely integrated with benefits or social security systems. Therefore, to avoid the benefits of radical tax reform being diluted, welfare reform ought to accompany tax reform to ensure that incentives to work and save are increased. Merely cutting taxes for some sections of the population may not increase incentives enough if the welfare system continues unchanged (Heath, 2006: 101).

Furthermore, researchers at the Harvard Business School conducted a case study of Slovakia's introduction of the flat tax. Their research led them to conclude:

> [T]he countries that have introduced a flat tax have all been in macroeconomic situations where something had to be done to foster growth and attract investments, which indicates a major trend for linking tax reform with, for instance, privatization and labor and welfare reforms. So existing evidence indicates that overhauling other parts of the public system, in order to afford a perceived cut in tax revenues through a flat tax implementation, is needed. This, however, does not indicate that the opposite is impossible. (Lagace, 2007)

How does one navigate the political issues created by the transition from a progressive to a flat tax? Economist Anthony Evans' seminal analysis of the spread of the flat tax throughout much of Central and Eastern Europe confirmed that, "interests matter" (Evans, 2007: 36; also Evans, 2005, 2006) Neither should one underestimate the importance of a political culture that places tremendous value upon a particular, albeit skewed, definition of economic fairness. The Austrian economist Joseph A. Schumpeter suggested that the history of a nation's tax system charts that society's ideological evolution. For Schumpeter, "[t]he spirit of a people, its cultural level, its social structure, the deeds its policy may prepare—all this and more is written in its fiscal history" (Schumpeter, 1918/1954: 7).

In a comment on the political situation in the United States that is equally applicable to Canada, Rabushka does not think that, "politicians here want to defend the argument of rich people getting a tax cut" (Lazarus, 2007:C1) Laura Alfaro and her Harvard Business School colleagues explained that "[t]he case of Slovakia highlights the fact that the beliefs and views of a country on what is fair matter for the long-term sustainability of reforms" (Lagace, 2007). The political debate over personal income taxes is intense during campaign periods. At this time, candidates and their parties generally do not compete with one another over the income-tax rates; rather, they seduce voters with promises to introduce additional deductions and exemptions once elected to office.[22] Introducing a flat tax in North America or Western Europe, therefore, "would require a change of attitude in countries marked by a substantial history with progressive taxation ... Most certainly, the elimination of deductions and exemptions is a battle many politicians will not want to take on in the near future" (Lagace, 2007).

Hence, Epstein recommends a two-fold strategy (Epstein, 2004: 29). First, one should explain the long-term benefits to the public, including the effects on saving, investment, and economic growth over the next 15 to 20 years. One lesson culled from the European experience is that any changes to fundamental tax habits need to be thoroughly explained to the individuals and groups affected by the changes (Lagace, 2007). Second, the government should phase in the move to a single tax rate. Here, Epstein arguably understates the problematic nature of phased-in tax rate reductions. On the economic side, they create incentives for people to postpone economic activity. On the political side, there is a risk that the phase-in will be aborted.

Without question, mobilizing political support for radical change is much harder in North American and Western European nations than in the Central and Eastern European nations that are more inclined to radicalism (*Economist*, 2005b, April 14). Nevertheless, the international experience teaches us that these political hurdles are surmountable, even in Western Europe. For example, beginning in 1995 Iceland gradually reduced its personal income-tax rates from a high of 33% (excluding the impact of ubiquitous local income taxes). This followed a decade of reducing the corporate tax rate—from 45% to 18% between 1991 and 2001—which tripled corporate tax revenues. A decade of economic growth averaging 4% encouraged the government to go a step further (*Wall Street Journal*, 2007, March 12). Hence, in 2007 Iceland became the first Western European nation to adopt a flat tax for personal income.[23] Iceland today taxes all personal income at a flat rate

---

22 ◆ Competition over the income-tax rates did happen, albeit briefly, in Canada. In 1993, during its first national campaign, the Reform Party's policy platform proposed a flat tax.

23 ◆ For a recent discussion of the fiscal changes in Iceland, see Mitchell, 2007b.

of 22.75%, though local income taxes push the rate up to about 36%. Now, capital gains, dividends, interest, and rental incomes are taxed at a flat rate of 10% (Reynolds, 2007).

Perhaps, Canadian politicians may be converted to the flat tax if they can be convinced that the flat tax holds out the promise of higher revenues. As economist Niclas Berggren explained, politicians "see high revenues ... as valuable for sustaining profitable ties with supporters" (Berggren, 2003: 11). Certainly, political entrepreneurs who are prepared to campaign for efficiency-based tax reform can influence policy-making (Poterba, 1998: 395). In practice, economic research's polity utility depends on the presence of a political actor—or several—both willing and able to bring the research implications to a wide audience (Noll, 1989). Today, there exists abundant evidence of the flat tax's superiority and suitability. All that is missing is a confident Canadian leader with the political *nous* to recognize how eminently marketable is the flat tax.

The role of tax competition

While ideology and public choice will play a role, globalization may be the key to Canadian tax reform. Indeed, it is likely to be the force that leads to the flat tax in other industrialized nations. Simply stated, globalization has reduced impediments to cross-border economic activity. And this means that the proverbial geese with golden eggs have more freedom to find jurisdictions that welcome wealth creation.

Since 1980, top personal income-tax rates have fallen from an average of more than 65% in developed nations to about 40%. This drop of more than 25 percentage points is at least partially due to other nations playing catch-up in response to the tax-rate reductions under Reagan and Thatcher. Similarly, average corporate tax rates in the industrialized world have plummeted from about 48% in 1980 to about 28% today. Reagan and Thatcher got the ball rolling but Ireland's decision to drop its corporate rate from 50% to 12.5%—and the nation's subsequent economic boom—deserve most of the credit for the global shift to lower rates.

Even the global tax-reform revolution is at least partially inspired by competition among nations. As transition economies in Central and Eastern Europe compete for jobs and investment, they increasingly have opted for a flat tax as a way of making their economies more attractive. The only question is whether tax competition will help convince Canadian lawmakers to embrace sweeping reform. Already, moves to lower the corporate tax are being explicitly justified with tax-competition arguments. Policy-makers note that lower rates make Canada more appealing than the United States, which has one of the developed world's highest corporate tax rates.

In a global economy, tax competition is going to play an increasingly bigger role. Many governments in developed nations are concerned about jobs and investment flowing to India and China. As these countries continue to liberalize, the pressure for more market-friendly policy will become even more pronounced.

Tax policy is not the only lever to pull, but few policy choices are as dramatic as a flat tax. In one fell swoop, Canada could make itself a magnet for investors and entrepreneurs. And with tax rates likely to climb in the United States, a flat tax would send a powerful signal.

Conclusion

A century ago, the *New York Times* editorialized against the introduction of the progressive income tax. In a warning that has stood the test of time, the newspaper cautioned that "[w]hen men get in the habit of helping themselves to the property of others, they cannot be easily cured of it" (Moore, 2007: A12). Today, progressive personal income-tax rates make for a needlessly complex tax system. Increasingly, therefore, taxpayers ask if there is a realistic alternative to our wasteful, inefficient tax system. This chapter's answer is a resounding yes. A realistic, proven alternative exists—the flat tax—and its successful international application threatens to relegate the Canadian tax system to a second division of national tax codes.

The international flat-tax experience confounds Hettich and Winer's cynical assertion that it is possible to have a flat tax, or to have democracy, but not both (Hettich and Winer, 2005). The most telling signal, perhaps, of the flat tax's suitability to the modern capitalist economy is that no country that has introduced the flat tax has reversed course and re-adopted a progressive tax system.

Ninety-one years ago, H.L. Mencken wrote that "[d]emocracy is the theory that the common people know what they want, and deserve to get it good and hard" (Mencken, 1916: 19). In an expanding number of Western democracies, the common people want either to have or to keep the flat tax. One trusts that, in time, Canadian voters will allow the country's taxpayers to experience the flat tax for themselves.

References

Adams, Charles (2001). *For Good and Evil: The Impact of Taxes on the Course of Civilization.* Madison Books.

Aligica, P.D., and H. Terpe (2005). The Flat Tax Experiment: The Romanian Case. Working paper.

Atkinson, Anthony B. (2004). *Public Economics in Action: The Basic Income/Flat Tax Proposal.* Oxford University Press.

BBC (2007). Romanian Premier Says Economic Growth Goes On in Spite of Political Turmoil (May 8). BBC Monitoring Service.

Berggren, Niclas (2003). *The Frailty of Economic Reforms: Political Logic and Constitutional Lessons.* Ratio Institute Working Paper No. 1. Ratio Institute (Stockholm, Sweden).

Beschloss, Morris R. (2007). Russian Economy Swiftly Accelerating. *Desert Sun* (May 13). D3

Boston Globe (2005). Eastern Europe Embraces Flat Tax: Former Communist Nations See Revenue Rise, Cheating Decline (February 22). <http://www.boston.com/business/articles/2005/02/22/eastern_europe_embraces_flat_tax/>.

Brennan, G., and J.M. Buchanan (1980). *The Power to Tax: Analytical Foundations of a Fiscal Constitution.* Cambridge University Press.

Buchanan, J.M. (1987). Tax Reform as Political Choice. *Journal of Economic Perspectives* 1: 29–35.

Buchanan, James M., and Gordon Tullock (1962). *The Calculus of Consent.* University of Michigan Press.

Butler, Eamonn (2004). The Rich Will Pay More if You Tax Them at a Flat Rate. *The Business* (November 21). <http://www.adamsmith. org/think-piece/economy/the-rich-will-pay-more-if-you-tax-them-at-a-flat-rate-2004112163/>.

Canada, Department of Finance (2006). *Tax Expenditures and Evaluations: Government of Canada, 2006.* <http://www.fin.gc.ca/ taxexp/2006/taxexp2006_e.pdf>.

Chren, Martin (2006). The Slovakian Tax System: Key Features and Lessons for Policy Makers. *Prosperitas* 1, 6. <http://www. freedomandprosperity.org/Papers/slovakia/slovakia.shtml>.

Clemens, Jason, Joel Emes, and Rodger Scott (2003). The Flat Tax—A Model for Reform of Personal and Business Taxes. In Herbert Grubel (ed.), *Tax Reform in Canada: Our Path to Greater Prosperity* (The Fraser Institute): 53–76.

Cordato, Roy E., and Sheldon L. Richman (1986). Tax Rate vs. Tax Base: A Public Choice Perspective on the Consequences for the Growth of Government. *Journal of Libertarian Studies* 8, 1: 63–68.

de Vanssay, X., and Z.A. Spindler (1994). Is Tax Reform in the Public Interest? A Rent-Seeking Perspective. *Public Finance Quarterly* 22 1: 3–21.

DiLorenzo, T.J. (1985). The Rhetoric and Reality of Tax Reform. *Cato Journal* 5: 401–06.

Dow Jones Newswire (2007). Slovak 1Q GDP Growth below Forecasts but Still Solid (May 15).

Economist Intelligence Unit (2005). Romania Economy: Will the Tax Changes Fall Flat? (January 13). <www.viewswire.com/index. asp?layout=display_print&doc_id=1387942138>.

Economist (2000, February 24). Atonement Day. <http://www.economist.com/displaystory.cfm?story_id=285834>.

Economist (2005, March 3). Flat Is Beautiful. <http://www.economist.com/world/europe/displaystory.cfm?story_id=E1_PSTVRDD>.

Economist (2005, April 14a). The Case for Flat Taxes. <http://www.economist.com/business/displaystory.cfm?story_id=E1_PRGDSPT>.

Economist (2005, April 14b). The Flat-Tax Revolution (Editorial). <http://www.economist.com/opinion/displaystory.cfm?story_id=E1_PRGTTJD>.

Economist (2005, October 13). Estonia and Slovenia: When Small Is Beautifully Successful. <http://www.economist.com/world/europe/displaystory.cfm?story_id=5025737>.

Economist (2006, June 1). Slovakia and Serbia: A Tale of Two Slavic States. <http://www.economist.com/world/europe/displaystory.cfm?story_id=7008578>.

Economist (2006, December 13). The Dynamic Duo: Eastern Europe's Stars. <http://www.economist.com/world/europe/displaystory.cfm?story_id=8417995>.

Edwards, Chris (2005a). *Catching Up to Global Tax Reforms*. Cato Institute Tax & Budget Bulletin No. 28. Cato Institute.

Edwards, Chris (2005b). *Options for Tax Reform*. Cato Institute Policy Analysis No. 536. Cato Institute.

Emes, Joel, Jason Clemens, Patrick Basham, and Dexter Samida (2001). *Flat Tax: Principles and Issues*. Critical Issues Bulletin. The Fraser Institute.

Engels, Friedrich, and Karl Marx (1848). *Communist Manifesto.* Communist League, London.

Epstein, Richard A. (2004). *The Case for a Flat Tax.* New Zealand Business Roundtable.

EurActiv.com (2006, November 9). *Flat Tax.* <www.euractiv.com/en/ taxation/flat-tax/article-136190?>.

Evans, Anthony J. (2005). Ideas and Interests: The Flat Tax. *Open Republic* 1, 1. <http://www.openrepublic.org/open_ republic/20050701_vol1_no1/articles/20050619_ft.htm>.

Evans, Anthony J. (2006). The Spread of Economic Theology: The Flat Tax in Romania. *Romanian Economic and Business Review* 1, 1: 41–52.

Evans, Anthony J. (2007). *The Spread of the Flat Tax: A Comparative Study.* Mercatus Center.

Frontier Centre for Public Policy (2000). *Andrei Illarionov, Putin's Economics Advisor.* Frontier Centre for Public Policy (December 1). <http://www.fcpp.org/main/publication_detail. php?PubID=230class>.

Fund, John (2005). High Taxes Wither Away. *New York Sun* (March 1). <http://www.nysun.com/article/9874>.

Grabowski, Maciej, and Marcin Tomalak (2004). *Tax System Reforms in the Countries of Central Europe and the Commonwealth of Independent States.* <www.warsawvoice.pl/krynica2004/ Special%20Study.pdf>.

Grecu, Andrei (2004). *Flat Tax – The British Case.* Adam Smith Institute.

Grubel, Herbert (Ed.) (2003). *Tax Reform in Canada: Our Path to Greater Prosperity.* The Fraser Institute.

Gwartney, James, Robert Lawson, and William Easterly (2006). *Economic Freedom of the World: 2006 Annual Report.* The Fraser Institute.

Hall, Robert E., and Alvin Rabushka (2007). *The Flat Tax* (2nd edition). Hoover Institution. <http://www.hooverpress.org/productdetails.cfm?PC=1274>.

Hansen, Alicia (2006). *A Flat Tax for Costa Rica?* Tax Foundation (October 11) <http://www.taxfoundation.org/blog/show/1930.html>.

Heath, Allister (2006). *Flat Tax: Towards a British Model.* Taxpayers Alliance.

Henninger, Daniel (2006). Optimism Pays Off. *Wall Street Journal* (November 17). <http://www.opinionjournal.com/forms/printThis.html?id=110009259>.

Herbert, Nick (2005). A New Deal for the Poor. *Spectator* (March 17). <http://www.reform.co.uk/website/pressroom/articles.aspx?o=65>.

Hettich, W., and S.L. Winer (1985). Blueprints and Pathways: The Shifting Foundation of Tax Reform. *National Tax Journal* 38: 423–45.

Hettich, W., and S.L. Winer (1988). Economic and Political Foundations of Tax Structure. *American Economic Review* 78: 701–12.

Hettich, Walter, and Stanley L. Winer (2005). *Democratic Choice and Taxation: A Theoretical and Empirical Analysis.* Cambridge University Press.

Holcombe, Randall (1998). Tax Policy from a Public Choice Perspective. *National Tax Journal* 51(2): 359–71.

ING (2005). Flat Tax Update. *Directional Economics* (March).

Internal Revenue Service (2007). Forms and Publications. <http://www.irs.gov/formspubs/lists/0,,id=97817,00.html>, as of November 6, 2007.

Ionita, Sorin (2006). *The Truth about the Flat Tax*. SAR Policy Brief No. 18. Romanian Academic Society (SAR).

Ivanova, Anna, Michael Keen, and Alexander Klemm (2005). *The Russian Flat Tax Reform*. IMF Working Paper 0516. International Monetary Fund.

Kennedy, Simon (2007). Corporate Tax Cuts, Once Fought, Gain Favor in EU. *International Herald Tribune* (May 29): 5.

Kerr, Roger (2007). Another Budget of Missed Opportunities. *National Business Review* (May 18). <http://www.nzbr.org.nz/documents/articles/070518anotherbudget.htm>.

Kleinman, Mark (2007). Shadow Hangs over Success of Hong Kong. *Daily Telegraph* (June 30). <http://www.telegraph.co.uk/money/main.jhtml?xml=/money/2007/06/30/cchk130.xml>.

Konnov, Oleg (2007). Tax Relief. *The Lawyer* (May 14). <http://www.thelawyer.com/cgi-bin/item.cgi?ap=1&id=125834>.

Koza, Harry (2007). Russian Mortgage Market Undergoing a Revolution. *Globe and Mail* (May 11): B11.

Lagace, Martha (2007). *All Eyes on Slovakia's Flat Tax*. "Q&A with Laura Alfaro, Vincent Dessain, and Ane Damgaard Jensen." Harvard Business School. (April 30) <http://hbswk.hbs.edu/item/5653.html>.

Landler, Mark (2005). A Land of Northern Lights, Cybercafes and the Flat Tax. *New York Times* (December 21). <http://www.nytimes.com/2005/12/21/international/europe/21letter.html?_r=1&oref=slogin>.

Lazarus, David (2007). The Flat Tax: It's Simple, Alluring but One-Size-Fits-All Faces Skepticism, Too. *San Francisco Chronicle* (April 11): C1.

Leach, Graeme (2003). *The Negative Impact of Taxation on Economic Growth*. Reform.

Lee, D.R., and R.D. Tollison (1988). Optimal Taxation in a Rent-Seeking Environment. In C.K. Rowley, R.D. Tollison, and G. Tullock (eds), *The Political Economy of Rent Seeking* (Kluwer): 339–50.

Littlewood, Michael (2007). The Hong Kong Tax System: Key Features and Lessons for Policy Makers. *Prosperitas* 7, 2. <http://www.freedomandprosperity.org/Papers/hongkong/hongkong.shtml>.

Long, Simon (2007). One-Horse Race: A Special Report on Hong Kong. *The Economist* (June 30). <http://www.economist.com/specialreports/displaystory.cfm?story_id=9359188>.

Lynn, Matthew (2004). Eastern Europe Gives Taste of Flat-Tax Paradise. *Bloomberg News Service* (November 29). <http://www.bloomberg.com/apps/news?pid=10000039&refer=columnist_lynn&sid=aNSQHmLkk_Lw>.

McCaleb, T.S. (1985). Public Choice Perspectives on the Flat Tax Follies. *Cato Journal* 5:613–24.

McChesney, F.S. (1988). The Cinderella School of Tax Reform: A Comment on Rabushka. *Contemporary Policy Issues* 6: 65–69.

Muntean, Cristina (2007). Investors Undeterred by Romanian Politics. *Cross Border* (May 28). *CBW/Czech Business Weekly*. <http://www.cbw.cz/phprs/2007052804.html>.

Mencken, H.L. (1916). *A Little Book in C Major*. John Lane.

Mitchell, Daniel J. (2003a). Russia's Flat-Tax Miracle. *Scripps Howard News Service* (March 24). <http://www.heritage.org/Press/Commentary/ed032403.cfm>.

Mitchell, Daniel J. (2003b). Slovakia: Hong Kong of Eastern Europe. *Washington Times* (November 29).

Mitchell, Daniel J. (2005). Will Europe's Flat Tax Revolution Spread from East to West? *European Affairs* (Fall).

Mitchell, Daniel J. (2006). A Flat-Out Winner for Tax Reform. *Freedom Works* (January 5). < http://www.freedomworks.org/informed/issues_template.php?issue_id=2468>.

Mitchell, Daniel (2007a). Baltic Beacon. *Wall Street Journal Europe* (June 20). <http://www.cato.org/pub_display.php?pub_id=8378>.

Mitchell, Daniel J. (2007b). *Iceland Comes in From the Cold with Flat Tax Revolution* (March 21). Cato Institute. <http://www.cato.org/pub_display.php?pub_id=8155>.

Mitchell, Daniel J. (2007c). The Global Flat Tax Revolution. *Cato Policy Report* (July/August). <http://www.cato.org/pubs/policy_report/v29n4/cpr29n4-1.pdf>.

Mongabay.com (1986–1998). Estonia - Economy. <http://www.mongabay.com/reference/country_studies/estonia/ECONOMY.html>.

Moore, Stephen (2007). Supply Side: Those April Blues. *Wall Street Journal* (April 13): A12.

Morris R. Beschloss (2007). Russian Economy Swiftly Accelerating. *The Desert Sun* (May 13). <http://tinyurl.com/35pv2j> [available by purchase or subscription only].

Noll, Roger G. (1989). Comment. *Brookings Papers on Economic Activity: Micreconomics:* 48–58.

Pirie, Madsen (2005). Missing the Point. Blog (May 20). Adam Smith Institute. <http://www.adamsmith.org/blog-archive/001319.php>.

Poterba, James M. (1998). Public Finance and Public Choice. *National Tax Journal* 51, 2: 391–96.

Rabushka, Alvin (1979). *Hong Kong: A Study in Economic Freedom.* University of Chicago.

Rabushka, Alvin (2004). *The Flat Tax at Work in Russia: Year Three.* Comments, Essays, and Speeches. Hoover Institution. <http://www.hoover.org/research/russianecon/essays/5144587.html>.

Rabushka, Alvin (2005a). *A Competitive Flat Tax May Spread to Lithuania* (March 24). Comments, Essays, Speeches. Hoover Institution. <http://www.hoover.org/research/russianecon/essays/5085376.html>.

Rabushka, Alvin (2005b). *The Flat Tax at Work in Russia: Year Four, 2004* (January 26). Comments, Essays, and Speeches. Hoover Institution. <http://www.hoover.org/research/russianecon/essays/5146322.html>.

Rabushka, Alvin (2005c). *The Flat Tax Gathers Momentum in Western Europe.* Comments, Essays, and Speeches. Hoover

Institution. <http://www.hoover.org/research/russianecon/essays/5084596.html>.

Rabushka, Alvin (2005d). *The Flat Tax Spreads to Georgia* (January 3) Comments, Essays, and Speeches. Hoover Institution. <http://www.hoover.org/research/russianecon/essays/5146252.html>.

Reynolds, Alan (1999). *The Hong Kong Tax System*. Hudson Institute.

Reynolds, Alan (2005). *Hong Kong's Excellent Taxes*. TownHall.com (June 2). <http://www.cato.org/pub_display.php?pub_id=3793>.

Reynolds, Neil (2007). No Stopping Flat-Tax Juggernaut. *Globe and Mail* (May 2): B2.

ROMPRES (2007). The Reform Carried Out by the Previous Governments (May 7). *National Press Agency/ROMPRES*. <http://www.rompres.ro/>.

Rowley, C.K., R.D. Tollison, and G. Tullock, eds. (1988). *The Political Economy of Rent Seeking*. Kluwer.

Schumpeter, J.A. (1918/1954). The Crisis of the Tax State. In A.T. Peacock, R. Turvey, W.F. Stolper, and E. Henderson, eds., *International Economic Papers* 4, 34: 5–38.

Simeonova, Sofia (2007). A Quarter of Europe Swept by Tax Reform Fever. *PARI Daily* (April 26).

Slate, Daniel D. (2005). Fair and Flat: The European Flat Tax Revolution. *Stanford Review*, 35, 4. <http://www.stanfordreview.org/Archive/Volume_XXXV/Issue_4/Foreign_Affairs/affairs1.shtml>.

Spindler, Zane, and M. Walker (1988). Canadian Tax Reform as Public Choice. *Contemporary Policy Issues* 6, 4: 70–84.

Srdoc-Samy, Natasha (2007). Flat-Taxers Show the Way. *Balkan Investigative Reporting Network (BIRN)* (May 16). <http://www.birn.eu.com/en/83/10/2913/>.

Stokey, N.L., and S. Rebelo (1995). Growth Effects of Flat-Rate Taxes. *Journal of Political Economy* 103, 3: 1011–25.

Tax History Museum (1997–2006). *1861–1865: The Civil War.* <http://www.tax.org/Museum/1861-1865.htm>.

Trefgarne, George (2005). The Flat Tax Secrets that Worried Brown Did Not Want Us to See. *Daily Telegraph* (August 19). <http://www.telegraph.co.uk/news/main.jhtml?xml=/news/2005/08/19/ntax119.xml>.

Tzortzis, Andreas (2005). Flat-Tax Movement Stirs Europe. *Christian Science Monitor* (March 8). <http://www.csmonitor.com/2005/0308/p01s03-woeu.htm>.

Underhill, William (2007). Eastern Europeans Have Faith in Flat Tax. *Newsweek* (February 21). <http://www.msnbc.msn.com/id/6959820/site/newsweek/print/1/displaymode/1098/>.

van Velthoven, B., and F. van Winden (1991). A Positive Model of Tax Reform. *Public Choice* 72: 61–86.

Ventura, G. (1999). Flat Tax Reform: A Quantitative Exploration. *Journal of Economic Dynamics and Control* 23: 1425–58.

Wagner, R.E. (1985). Normative and Positive Foundations of Tax Reform. *Cato Journal* 5: 385–99.

Wall Street Journal (2005, October 7). The World Is Flat. Editorial. <http://online.wsj.com/article/SB112864535887162338.html>.

Wall Street Journal (2007, March 12). Iceland's Laffer Curve. Editorial. <http://online.wsj.com/article/SB117330772978430098.html>.

Wall Street Journal (2007, April 17). The Czechs Are Flat. Editorial: A18.

Winer, Stanley L., and Walter Hettich (1998). What Is Missed If We Leave Out Collective Choice in the Analysis of Taxation. *National Tax Journal* 52, 2: 373–89.

Chapter 5

A Flat Tax for Canada

Alvin Rabushka & Niels Veldhuis

Canada's federal and provincial tax systems are impeding the country's ability to reach its full economic potential. Most significantly, Canada's personal and corporate income taxes reduce economic growth by creating strong disincentives to work hard, save, invest, and engage in entrepreneurial activities. In addition, individuals and businesses incur large costs to comply with Canada's tax code and pay for the government's tax-collection system. As a result of these costs and distorted incentives, Canadians would benefit considerably from a more economically friendly, efficient, income-tax system.

This chapter presents a proposal for a thorough reform of Canada's federal and provincial income-tax systems. Specifically, we propose an integrated flat tax for Canada based on a model first crafted for the United States by Robert E. Hall and Alvin Rabushka of the Hoover Institution.[1] The proposed Canadian flat tax would significantly improve the incentives to engage in productive economic behavior and reduce the costs to comply with and administer the tax system while raising the same amount of revenue as the current system.

---

1 ◆ See Robert E. Hall and Alvin Rabushka, *The Flat Tax,* Second Edition (Hall and Rabushka, 2007). Dr. Rabushka previously proposed a flat tax for Canada in *Reforming the White Paper on Tax Reform* (Rabushka, 1987). The authors thank Milagros Palacios for her able assistance with the calculations presented in this chapter.

The first section of the chapter evaluates the simplicity, efficiency, and fairness of Canada's current income-tax system relative to that of a flat-tax system. Section 2 provides an overview of the Hall-Rabushka flat tax. Section 3 presents a flat tax for Canada based on the Hall-Rabushka proposal. Section 4 discusses the likely impact of a flat tax on the Canadian economy.

1 ◆ The simplicity, efficiency, and fairness of Canada's income-tax system

In 2006, Canadian governments received nearly half of total tax revenues from income and profit taxes (personal and corporate income taxes).[2] To understand the need to reform this significant revenue source, it is important to highlight some of the failures of Canada's current income-tax system and show the remedies offered by a flat tax. This section evaluates Canada's current income-tax system using three criteria typically used to evaluate tax policy: simplicity, efficiency, and fairness (equity).

Simplicity

Few Canadians would defend the current income-tax system for its simplicity. Canadians spend a significant amount of time and money maintaining records, filing reports, and undertaking tax planning as a result of Canada's complex tax code. Canadian governments also expend significant resources collecting taxes and enforcing tax regulations. The estimated total compliance and administrative costs in Canada were between $18.9 billion and $30.8 billion in 2005; between $585 and $955 for each Canadian.[3]

The Hall-Rabushka flat tax proposed below would significantly reduce the complexity of Canada's tax system by reducing the number

---

2 ◆ See chapter 2, Not All Taxes Are Created Equal, for a detailed discussion of Canada's tax mix.

3 ◆ See chapter 3, Compliance and Administrative Costs of Taxation in Canada. It is important to note that these estimates also include property and sales taxes.

of tax forms and eliminating nearly all exemptions, deductions, and credits in the current system. The simplification of the tax system achieved through a flat tax would significantly reduce both compliance and administrative costs for Canadians. In addition, a significant portion of Canada's tax industry, including accountants and lawyers, would be redeployed to other, more productive uses.

Efficiency

An efficient tax system raises the required amount of revenues while minimizing economic distortions caused by the taxes. Distortions emerge because taxes alter the incentives for productive economic behavior such as savings, investment, work effort, and entrepreneurship. Chapter 3, Not All Taxes Are Created Equal, explains how different types of taxes influence economic behavior and presents research that shows business and personal income taxes are among the most inefficient taxes because they penalize productive economic activities. On the other hand, consumption-based taxes are found to be most efficient. Unfortunately, Canada relies most heavily on the most inefficient types of taxes.

The Hall-Rabushka flat tax would significantly improve the efficiency of Canada's income-tax system. First, the Hall-Rabushka flat tax is entirely based on the principle of taxing consumption rather than income. That is, the flat tax is based on consumption because all savings and investment activities are exempt from taxation. Individuals and families would only be taxed on the portion of their income they consume or take out of the economy. Money put back into the economy in the form of savings and investments would be exempt from the flat tax. The result is that a Hall-Rabushka flat tax is essentially a consumption tax because it is levied on income that is spent rather than saved.

The Hall-Rabushka proposal also reduces distortions through the elimination of graduated or progressive personal income-tax rates, replacing them with a single-rate tax. Evidence from economic research indicates that increasing marginal tax rates penalizes work effort, saving, investing, and other productive economic activities.[4]

---

4 ◆ See chapter 1, The Impact of Taxes on Economic Behavior.

Another rather unknown distortion is created by Canada's business income-tax system. That is, both federal and provincial governments offer reduced business income-tax rates to eligible small businesses, which has resulted in steep increases in statutory business income-tax rates as businesses grow. Economic research indicates that such increases in business income-tax rates create a powerful barrier, or disincentive, to growth and expansion.[5]

Finally, Canada's current income-tax system produces distortions as a result of numerous tax incentives that change the relative prices of different goods or activities, making some more attractive than others. These tax incentives distort economic decisions including the allocation of important resources such as labor and capital (buildings, machinery and equipment). Consider for example the generous tax credits investors receive for contributing to Labour Sponsored Venture Capital Funds.[6] Since these credits are not available to investors of private, non-labor funds, the tax credit partially substitutes for a rate of return. As a result, Canadians are investing in tax-subsidized labor funds to get generous tax credits despite the extraordinarily poor performance of these labor-sponsored funds.

Fairness

While a flat tax would significantly improve the efficiency and simplicity of the current tax system, debate surrounding flat taxes often results in concerns about fairness (equity). Fairness or equity refers to both horizontal equity and vertical equity.

Horizontal equity

Horizontal equity requires that individuals and households with similar incomes face similar tax burdens. Unfortunately, Canada's current income-tax system fails to achieve horizontal equity as some forms of income (i.e. certain fringe benefits) go untaxed while others (i.e. dividend income) are subject to double taxation. Consider, for example, that corporations pay dividends to shareholders after the 21.0% federal and

---

5 ◆ For a detailed analysis, see Clemens and Veldhuis, 2005.

6 ◆ For a detailed analysis, see Cumming and Godin, 2007.

applicable provincial corporate income taxes on earnings. Individuals must then declare the dividends as personal income and pay federal income taxes at rates up to 19.6% (see table 5.1). In addition, when shares (common stock) of the business are sold, the individual must pay up to 14.5% federal income tax on any capital gains that are realized.

Interest payments to individuals, on the other hand, are a deductible expense for businesses and taxable at federal personal income-tax rates of up to 29.0%. In other words, payments made by businesses to bond holders are tax deductible while payments to shareholders in the form of dividends are not. The result is that the combined corporate and personal income-tax rate on interest income is lower than that on dividends, which means debt receives preferential treatment relative to equity under the current tax system.

The differential taxes on income from investments distort decisions both by investors seeking investment opportunities and by businesses that distribute earnings. In addition, the differential taxes created to integrate corporate and personal income taxes add considerable complexity to Canadian's income-tax system. Table 5.1 presents the federal statutory personal income-tax rates (and thresholds) on dividends, capital gains, interest income and ordinary (wage) income for 2007.

Table 5.1: Federal statutory personal income tax rates and thresholds (2007)

Bracket	Interest and ordinary income	Capital gains	Canadian dividends
$120,887 and over	29.0%	14.5%	19.6%
$74,357 to $120,886	26.0%	13.0%	15.8%
$37,178 to $74,356	22.0%	11.0%	10.8%
$9,601 to $37,177	15.0%	7.5%	2.1%
$0 to $9,600	0.0%	0.0%	0.0%

Note: The basic personal exemption of $9,600, the amount that all Canadians can earn without paying federal income tax, is not cumulative across the different forms of income.

Source: Canada, Department of Finance, 2007b; PricewaterhouseCoopers, 2007; calculations by the authors.

Another violation of the principal of horizontal equity in the current income-tax system is the bias towards two-income families and against one-income families. That is, families with equal incomes pay different amounts of income tax depending on how the income is distributed within the family.[7] The bias results from the fact that the single-earner faces higher income-tax rates than a multiple-earner family with the same income. In addition, the bias widens as family income increases and also if the family contains dependant children. Child-care expenses, amounts paid to have someone look after a child, are deductible from taxable income while child-care expenses cannot be claimed if services are provided by one of the child's parents.[8]

Vertical equity

Vertical equity is based on the notion that individuals and families with higher incomes should have to pay higher fractions of their incomes in taxes. The principle of vertical equity is most often used to justify Canada's graduated (or "progressive") income-tax rates. Table 5.2 shows federal and provincial personal income-tax brackets and rates for 2007. The federal government and all provinces, with the exception of Alberta, maintain personal income-tax rates that increase with individual income.

It is important, however, not to equate increasing personal income-tax rates with progressivity. Progressivity simply means that the share of income one pays in taxes increases as one earns more income. To achieve progressivity it is not necessary to have increasing marginal personal income-tax rates.[9] Indeed, one of the primary benefits of flat or single-rate taxes is that they eliminate the negative impact caused by increasing

---

7 ◆ In Canada, all individuals must file income taxes separately regardless of marital status or living arrangement whereas married couples in the United States can file jointly or separately and the US tax system encourages joint filing through many tax incentives.

8 ◆ See Veldhuis and Clemens, 2004 for a complete analysis.

9 ◆ A marginal tax rate refers to the tax rate on the last dollar of income earned while an average tax rate is the fraction of total income paid in taxes. See chapter 1, The Impact of Taxes on Economic Behavior, for a detailed explanation of average and marginal tax rates.

Table 5.2: Federal & provincial personal income-tax rates and brackets, 2007

	Tax brackets ($)	Rates (%)	Surtax (% of provincial tax payable)
Federal	0–37,178	15.0	
	37,179–74,357	22.0	
	74,358–120,887	26.0	
	Over 120,887	29.0	
Newfoundland & Labrador	0–29,886	9.6	4.5% on amounts over $7,102
	29,887–59,772	15.0	
	Over 59,772	17.3	
Prince Edward Island	0–31,368	9.8	10% on amounts over $8,850
	31,369–62,739	13.8	
	Over 62,739	16.7	
Nova Scotia	0–29,589	8.8	10% on amounts over $10,000
	29,590–59,179	15.0	
	59,180–93,000	16.7	
	Over 93,000	17.5	
New Brunswick	0–34,185	10.1	N/A
	34,186–68,373	15.5	
	68,374–111,161	16.8	
	Over 111,161	18.0	
Québec*	0–29,289	16.0	N/A
	29,290–58,595	20.0	
	Over 58,595	24.0	
Ontario	0–35,487	6.1	20% on amounts over $4,100
	35,488–70,976	9.2	36% on amounts over $5,172
	Over 70,976	11.2	
Manitoba	0–30,543	10.9	N/A
	30,544–65,000	13.0	
	Over 65,000	17.4	
Saskatchewan	0–37,404	11.0	N/A
	37,405–109,729	13.0	
	Over 109,729	15.0	
Alberta		10.0	
British Columbia	0–34,396	5.7	N/A
	34,397–68,793	8.7	
	68,794–78,983	11.1	
	78,984–95,909	13.0	
	Over 95,909	14.7	

Notes: Bracket and rates are for income above a tax-free exemption. See table 5.7 for provincial and federal exemption amounts. *Québec's tax rates are not adjusted for abatements.

Source: Canada, Department of Finance, 2007a, 2007b; Canada Revenue Agency, 2007a; PricewaterhouseCoopers, 2007.

marginal tax rates while maintaining progressivity.[10] That is, with a flat or single-rate tax progressivity is achieved while avoiding the disincentives for individuals to engage in productive economic behavior present with increasing marginal rates. Under a flat or single-rate tax, progressivity is achieved through a personal allowance or exemption, an amount of income all individuals are permitted to earn tax-free. While the exemption is available to individuals at all income levels, they constitute a much larger portion of income for Canadians earning a low or modest income.

To understand how a personal allowance or exemption leads to a progressive tax system, it is instructive to examine personal income taxes in Alberta. Alberta has a single-rate personal income tax of 10% applicable to income over $15,435, Alberta's personal exemption. In other words, the personal income-tax rate in Alberta stays constant at 10% regardless of an individual's income, provided it is above $15,435. To examine the degree of progressivity in Alberta's tax regime one must examine average tax rates. That is, what portion of income does an individual pay in personal income taxes. Figure 5.1 and table 5.3 show the average income tax paid at various income levels in Alberta.[11] Because the personal exemption constitutes a much higher portion of income for those earning a lower income, only a small portion of their total income is subject to tax. As a result, average tax rates for those earning a lower income are substantially lower than for those earning a higher income.

Conclusion

Canada's current income tax system is neither simple, efficient, nor equitable (fair). Taxpayers spend significant resources complying with and financing the administration of our complex tax system. The tax

---

10 ◆ There is a critical difference between an integrated flat tax and single-rate personal income tax. An integrated flat tax does not simply replace multiple personal income-tax rates with a single tax rate. Rather, under an integrated flat tax, all types of income, personal and business, are uniformly taxed at one rate and only taxed once. See below for further explanation.

11 ◆ This example is for illustrative purposes only. Actual marginal tax rates will be affected by income-tested benefits and credits. See page 181 for further discussion.

Figure 5.1: *Marginal and average tax rates in Alberta, 2007*

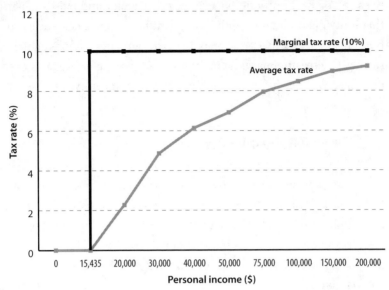

Source: Table 5.3.

Table 5.3: *Average Tax Rates in Alberta*

Personal income ($)	Taxable income ($)	Tax Paid ($)	Average tax rate (%)
15,000	—	—	0.0%
20,000	4,565	457	2.3%
30,000	14,565	1,457	4.9%
40,000	24,565	2,457	6.1%
50,000	34,565	3,457	6.9%
75,000	59,565	5,957	7.9%
100,000	84,565	8,457	8.5%
150,000	134,565	13,457	9.0%
200,000	184,565	18,457	9.2%

Notes: Taxable income is calculated by subtracting the basic personal exemption of $15,435 from total income (column 1). Taxpayers may also be eligible for the spousal or equivalent-to-spouse exemptions. Data and calculations are for illustrative purposes only and do not include the impact of income-tested benefits and credits on magrinal tax rates.

Source: Alberta, Ministry of Finance, 2007; calculations by the authors.

system also creates damaging economic distortions that alter the incentives to engage in productive economic behavior and fails to ensure that individuals and households with similar incomes face similar tax burdens. Finally, while progressivity in the current system is achieved through increasing marginal tax rates, a flat or single-rate tax system can do so without having a negative impact on incentives.

2 ◆ The Hall-Rabushka flat tax

This section provides a brief overview of the flat-tax reform proposed by Robert E. Hall and Alvin Rabushka of the Hoover Institution (henceforth called the Hall-Rabushka flat tax), which was first proposed in 1981. It is perhaps the most influential flat-tax proposal put forth and has formed the basis for a host of international flat-tax reforms.[12]

The Hall-Rabushka flat tax is based on a single rate of tax for all sources of income; it does not simply replace multiple personal income-tax rates with a single tax rate.[13] Rather, the Hall-Rabushka proposal is an integrated flat tax wherein all types of income, personal and business, are uniformly taxed at one rate and only taxed once. As mentioned above, under Canada's current income-tax system certain types of income such as some fringe benefits are not taxed at all while other sources of income such as dividends and capital gains are taxed more than once and/or at differing rates.[14] In addition, the Hall-Rabushka

---

12 ◆ The following jurisdictions have single-rate or flat taxes (in order of enactment): Jersey, Hong Kong, Guernsey, Estonia, Latvia, Lithuania, Russia, Serbia, Slovakia, Ukraine, Iraq, Romania, Georgia, Iceland, Mongolia, Kyrgyzstan, Macedonia, Montenegro, and Bulgaria. See chapter 4, Lessons from Abroad: Flat Tax in Practice, for further details.

13 ◆ An example of single-rate tax reform occurred in Alberta in 2001 when the province introduced a 10% single personal income-tax rate to replace the existing multiple-rate structure. In addition, in 2000, the Canadian Alliance (the precursor to the Conservative Party) proposed a tax reform that would replace the three federal statutory personal income-tax rates with one rate (see Solberg, 2000).

14 ◆ For a detailed description of Canada's personal and business tax systems including the taxation of dividends and capital gains, see Treff and Perry, 2005.

flat tax significantly alters the tax base through the elimination of most tax credits, deductions, and exemptions.[15] Simply replacing multiple personal income-tax rates with one single rate retains differential tax rates on different types of income and the tax credits, exemptions, and deductions contained in the current system. The Hall-Rabushka flat tax is therefore a broad and comprehensive reform of the personal and business income-tax systems.

The Hall-Rabushka flat tax is an integrated system in that it applies the same tax rate to both business and individuals. All income is classified into either business income or wages (including salaries and pensions) and, as is currently the case, businesses and individuals would complete separate tax returns. The two major components of the Hall-Rabushka flat-tax proposal, the individual wage tax and the business tax, are discussed below.

The individual wage tax

Under Hall-Rabushka model, the personal income-tax system is replaced by the individual wage tax. It is important to note that the individual wage tax is not a separate tax system as is currently the case with personal income taxes but rather one of the two main parts of an integrated system. The individual wage tax applies only to income that employers pay as cash to their employees. That is, only wages, salaries, and pension benefits are deemed personal income and subject to the individual wage tax. Income from dividends, capital gains, interest, or in the form of benefits such as pension contributions are not subject to the individual wage tax because, as is discussed below, they are taxed at the business level.[16]

---

15 ◆ The tax base is the income (after deductions and exemptions) upon which the tax is levied. A broadening or widening of the tax base means that more income has been made subject to income tax.

16 ◆ The individual wage tax makes use of the current tax withholding system. Technically, the Hall-Rabushka flat tax could be put into operation without requiring individuals to submit tax forms. One of the primary reasons for the individual wage tax is that it requires taxpayers to calculate annually the amount of their wages sent to governments, thereby making it more difficult for advocates of increased government spending to promise new benefits without higher taxes.

The Hall-Rabushka flat tax would result in a dramatically simplified tax return for individuals and families. All that would be required is to sum income from wages, salaries, and retirement benefits minus the basic personal exemption (the amount of income individuals can earn tax free) to calculate taxable income. This amount is then multiplied by one rate to determine the individual or family tax bill for the year.[17] The amount withheld by employers is then compared to the amount owed to calculate whether the taxpayer is owed a refund or payment is due. The individual wage tax has no tax credits, deductions, or additional exemptions. In other words, the myriads of tax credits and deductions present in the current system and the attendant complicated and time-consuming paperwork are eliminated.

The business tax

The main purpose of the business tax under the Hall-Rabushka flat tax is to collect tax on income produced by businesses. It is critical to note that the business tax is not intended to tax businesses as businesses do not pay tax, only people do.[18] The owners of a business owe tax on the income produced by the business and the goal of the business tax is to collect the tax at the source of the income.

The business tax is a comprehensive tax on the income that businesses generate. All of the income derived from the sales of goods and services is subject to the business tax, minus a few deductions.[19] First, businesses are permitted to deduct the cost of all the goods and services purchased from other businesses and used as inputs in the production process. The deduction of inputs is permitted because the business tax is collected from the sellers of these inputs. Businesses can also deduct wages, salaries, and pensions as they are taxed under the

---

17 ◆ Hall and Rabushka propose a 19% integrated flat tax for the United States.

18 ◆ The cost of business taxation cannot be borne by a business since it is simply a legal arrangement between two or more parties to engage in an economic endeavor. Put differently, a piece of paper, albeit a legal one, cannot incur a tax. See Clemens and Veldhuis, 2003.

19 ◆ Financial income typically referred to as passive business income in the current tax system is not subject to the business tax.

individual wage tax described above. Lastly, businesses are permitted to deduct the full value of all capital investments (buildings, equipment, and land) in the year of purchase. The remainder of income is taxed at the same rate as the individual wage tax.

One of the central tenets of the Hall-Rabushka flat tax is to tax business income only once; the Hall-Rabushka flat tax eliminates the double taxation of business income in the current system.[20] To this end, businesses are not permitted to deduct interest payments or any other payments to owners (fringe benefits) in the form of expenses. The rationale for excluding these types of deductions and thus forcing the business to pay tax on them is to ensure that they are taxed only once. The income individuals and families receive from businesses is exempt from personal taxation (i.e. individual wage tax) because it has already been taxed at the business level.

Perhaps the largest single reform under Hall-Rabushka is the deductibility of the full value of all capital investments (buildings, machinery and equipment, and land) in the year of purchase. Businesses are currently able to write-off or deduct the cost of investing in new capital incrementally. That is, each year over a government-determined period, businesses are permitted to deduct a percentage of the total cost of purchasing plants and equipment. Under the Hall-Rabushka flat tax, the entire cost of capital is deducted as an expense in the year of purchase. Thus, depreciation schedules and the bureaucracy, both private (accountants and lawyers) and public (government revenue officials) are eliminated. In addition, there would be no conflict over whether the purchase of certain types of equipment are considered investments or expenses since Hall-Rabushka considers all such expenditures as expenses.

The taxable income computed after the deduction of input costs, wages and salaries, and capital investments bears little resemblance

---

20 ◆ As discussed above, debt receives preferential treatment relative to equity under the current tax system. Payments made by business to its bond holders are tax deductible while payments to shareholders in the form of dividends are not. Thus, by eliminating the tax deductibility of interest payments, the Hall-Rabushka flat-tax reform program eliminates preferential treatment of debt financing.

to what we now typically label "business profit." Therefore, the business tax should not be considered as a tax on profit. Consider a business that is having a successful year in terms of sales and revenue but is making significant capital investments. The business could have negative business income and thus negative business tax in a year in which it was performing well. The Hall-Rabushka proposal allows businesses to carry forward the negative business tax indefinitely and apply it to years in which the business has positive business tax. To minimize the impact that carrying forward a negative business tax would have on investment decisions made by businesses, the value carried would increase at the market rate of interest. Without allowing amounts carried forward to earn the market rate of interest, businesses might reduce their investment to ensure zero taxable income rather than negative taxable income since any money left over from reduced investment can alternatively be invested at the market rate by the business.

Conclusion

The Hall-Rabushka flat tax is a proposal for an entirely new income-tax system with a low rate on a broad definition of income in which all income would be taxed only once. All distortions currently caused by increasing marginal rates and special tax incentives would be eliminated. And as a result of a personal exemption, the tax would be fair and progressive with the percentage of income paid in taxes increasing with income.

3 ◆ A Canadian flat tax

This section presents an integrated flat tax for Canada, modeled on the framework of the Hall-Rabushka flat tax outlined above. The flat tax is revenue-neutral in that it would generate the same revenue as Canada's current corporate and individual taxes on income and profit. The first part of this section presents the federal flat tax and the second presents flat-tax calculations to replace personal and corporate income taxes in each Canadian province.

Federal flat tax

In 2006, the federal government collected $142.1 billion in personal and corporate income-tax revenues (table 5.4, line 14). To generate the equivalent amount of revenue from a Hall-Rabushka flat tax would require a rate of 15.0%. Calculations of the revenue-neutral federal flat tax are provided in detail below. While the Hall-Rabushka flat tax is an integrated system in that it applies the same 15.0% to businesses and individuals, both groups would be required to complete separate tax returns.

Individual wage tax

Figure 5.2 gives an example of what the Canadian federal tax return for the individual wage tax would look like under the Hall-Rabushka flat tax. Unlike the numerous and interlinked tax forms of Canada's current income-tax system, only one form and a few basic calculations are needed to determine the amount of tax owing or refund due. Taxpayers would be required to report total wages, salaries, and pensions at the top of the form (lines 1 & 2); compute their personal exemption (lines 4a–4c); and multiply their taxable compensation (line 6) by the 15.0% flat-tax rate to compute the federal wage tax. The personal exemption for the 2006 tax year was $8,839 for individuals. Taxpayers are able to claim an additional exemption of up to $7,505 if, at any time in the year, they supported a spouse or common-law partner.[21] Likewise, taxpayers can claim an additional exemption (called the equivalent-to-spouse amount) of up to $7,505 if, at any time during the year, they were single, divorced, separated, or widowed and at that time supported a dependant.[22] Put differently, the maximum that Canadians would have been permitted to earn tax-free in 2006 is $16,334, the basic personal exemption plus either the spousal or equivalent-to-spouse amounts.

---

21 ◆ To claim the full amount, the spouse's wages, salaries, and pension income must have been $751 or less. If spousal income was greater than $751, but less than $8,256, the taxpayer is able to claim the difference.

22 ◆ A dependant is considered a child under 18; a parent or grandparent; or a person 18 years or older, mentally or physically infirm, related by blood, marriage, or adoption and living with the taxpayer.

Figure 5.2: Sample form for federal Individual Wage Tax

Form #1—Individual Wage Tax		Tax Year 2006
Your first name and initial	Last name	Your social insurance number
Present home address (number and street including apartment number or rural route)		Spouse's social insurance number
City or town, province and postal code		Your occupation
		Spouse's occupation

1 Wages and salary ... 1

2 Pension and retirement benefits ... 2

3 Total compensation (line 1 plus line 2) ... 3

4 Personal Exemption

  (a) Basic personal amount ($8,839) ... 4(a)

  (b) Spousal amount (maximum of $7,505) ... 4(b)

  (c) Equivalent-to-spouse amount (maximum of $7,505) ... 4(c)

5 Total personal exemption (line 4a plus line 4b and 4c) ... 5

6 Taxable compensation (line 3 less line 5, if positive; otherwise zero) ... 6

7 Federal Wage Tax (15% of line 6) ... 7

8 Tax withheld by employer ... 8

9 Tax due (line 7 less line 8, if positive) ... 9

10 Refund due (line 8 less line 7, if positive) ... 10

Most of the features of Canada's current personal income tax would disappear under the individual wage tax including taxes on capital gains (discussed in detail below), dividends, interest, and foreign income. In addition, this reform would eliminate almost all of the deductions, exemptions, and credits like child-care expenses, union dues, medical expenses, tuition and textbooks, trades-persons' tools expenses, public transit passes, and contributions to Retirement Savings Plans (discussed in detail below) that currently narrow the tax base and cause numerous distortions.

For approximately 85% of Canadian taxpayers, no more would be required to pay income taxes than filling out this simple form once a year.[23] The remaining 15% of Canadian taxpayers who are self employed would need to fill out a business tax form. To take advantage of the tax-free basic personal exemption, self-employed individuals would pay themselves a salary at least equal to the exemption and deduct the amount as salary or wages on their business tax forms. Thereafter, it would not matter if they paid themselves a salary equal to the rest of their business income or report it on their business form since the tax rate is the same on both.

It is important to reiterate that the individual wage tax is not a complete income tax on individuals as it only applies to wages, salaries, and pension benefits. Other income that individuals receive such as dividend and interest income is taxed at the source of the income (the business level).

Business tax

Figure 5.3 presents an example of what the federal tax form for the business tax would look like under the Hall-Rabushka flat tax. Every business from sole-proprietors to Canada's largest companies would be required to complete and file this simple form. Line 1, gross revenue from sales, is the dollar value of all of the goods and services sold by

---

23 ◆ In the 2005, the latest year for which detailed tax and income statistics are available, approximately 3.7 million tax filers recorded business, professional, commission, farming, fishing or rental income. This represents approximately 15.9% of total tax filers (Canada Revenue Agency, 2007b). In addition, Statistics Canada's *Labour Force Historical Review* estimates that self-employment was 15.2% of total employment in 2006.

Figure 5.3: Sample form for federal Business Tax

Form #2—Business Tax	Tax Year 2006
Name of business	Business number
Street address (number and street including apartment number or rural route)	Principal products sold or services provided
City or town, province and postal code	

1 Gross revenue from sales	1 _____
2 Allowable costs	
(a) Purchases of goods, services, and materials	2(a) _____
(b) Wages, salaries, and pensions	2(b) _____
(c) Purchases of capital equipment, structures, and land	2(c) _____
3 Total allowable costs (sum of lines 2(a), 2(b), and 2(c))	3 _____
4 Taxable income (line 1 less line 3)	4 _____
5 Federal business tax (15% of line 4)	5 _____
6 Carry forward from last year	6 _____
7 Interest on carry forward (X% of line 6)	7 _____
8 Carry forward into this year (line 6 plus line 7)	8 _____
9 Tax due (line 5 less line 8, if positive)	9 _____
10 Carry forward to next year (line 8 less line 5, if positive)	10 _____

the business. Lines 2a to 2c report all of the allowable costs the business is able to deduct from gross revenue, including the amount paid for the inputs bought from other businesses, total wages and salaries (including pension payments), and the amount paid for purchases of new and used capital equipment, buildings, and land. Line 4 reports the taxable income of the business.

Again, it is important to highlight that taxable income under the Hall-Rabushka flat tax bears almost no relation to what is typically considered business profit. When a business invests in new buildings or purchases machinery and equipment to expand future operations, the business may have negative taxable income. The negative income tax can be carried forward to future years when the business has positive taxable income. There would be no limit to the number of years that the businesses could carry forward their negative business tax and the amount carried forward would earn the market rate of interest. Lines 6 to 10 record the amount of tax that the business must pay or is permitted to carry forward.

Calculating the revenue-neutral federal flat tax rate

Table 5.4 presents a calculation of a revenue-neutral Hall-Rabushka flat tax for Canada at the federal level for 2006, the latest year for which detailed National Income and Expenditure Accounts data is available.[24] To estimate the individual wage and business-tax rates needed to match the federal personal and corporate income-tax revenues for 2006 ($142.1 billion; table 5.4, line 14), an estimate of the tax base for each tax is needed.[25]

The tax base for the individual wage tax is the sum of wages, salaries, and pension benefits less total personal exemptions (allowances).[26]

---

24 ◆ The Income and Expenditure Accounts (IEA) are produced by Statistics Canada and give a comprehensive statistical picture of Canada's economy. See http://www.statcan.ca for more information.

25 ◆ The tax base is the income (after deductions and exemptions) upon which the tax is levied.

26 ◆ Other than the personal exemption (the amount of income all individuals are permitted to earn tax-free), the individual wage tax has no tax credits, deductions, or additional exemptions.

Table 5.4: Estimated revenues from a flat tax compared with current revenues from federal personal and corporate income taxes, 2006

Line	Income or revenue	Millions of dollars
1	Gross domestic product	1,439,291
2	Indirect business tax (VAT plus excises)	109,567
3	Income in GDP, but not in tax base	34,997
4	Wages, salaries, and pensions	721,536
5	Investment	174,790
6	Business-tax base (line 1 minus lines 2 through 5)	398,401
7	**Business-tax revenue (15.0% of line 6)**	**59,696**
8	Personal exemptions	171,344
9	Wage-tax base (line 4 less line 8)	550,192
10	**Wage-tax revenue (15.0% of line 9)**	**82,439**
11	Total flat-tax revenue (line 7 plus line 10)	142,135
12	2006 federal individual income-tax revenue	107,406
13	2006 corporate income-tax revenue	34,729
14	**Total actual revenue (line 12 plus line 13)**	**142,135**

Sources: Canada Revenue Agency, 2007b; Statistics Canada, 2007b, 2007c, 2007d, 2007e; Canada, Department of Finance (2007c), Tax Expenditures and Evaluations 2006; federal and provincial budgets, 2006, various jurisdictions; calculations by the authors.

In 2006, total wages, salaries, and pensions in Canada amounted to \$721.5 billion (table 5.4, line 4). The total value of the personal exemptions (basic personal, spousal, and equivalent-to-spouse exemptions) amounted to \$171.3 billion in 2006 (table 5.4, line 8).[27] The tax base for the individual wage tax is estimated at \$550.2 billion (table 5.4, line 9).

The tax base for the business tax is total revenue from the sale of goods and services less purchases of inputs from other firms; wages, salaries, and pensions paid to workers; and purchases of capital (plant, equipment, and land). Gross Domestic Product (GDP), the total value of goods and services produced in the Canadian economy, is used to estimate total revenue from the sale of goods and services. However, GDP must be adjusted for indirect business taxes that are included in GDP but not should be included in the business tax base (table 5.4, line 2). Indirect business taxes include all taxes that represent a business cost (i.e. sales taxes, excise taxes, and import duties) minus subsidies from government to businesses.[28] In addition, GDP includes an estimate of the rental value of houses owned and lived in by families (imputed rental income of owner-occupied housing), which must be removed to calculate the business tax base (table 5.4, line 3). Finally, businesses are able to fully deduct wages, salaries, and pensions (table 5.4, line 4) and the amount spent on structures (buildings), machinery, and equipment (table 5.4, line 5). The tax base for the business tax (GDP less indirect business taxes, imputed rents, wages, salaries and pensions, and investment) is estimated at \$398.4 billion (table 5.4, line 6).

In 2006, the federal government collected \$142.1 billion in personal and corporate income-tax revenues (table 5.4, line 14). To generate

---

27 ◆ The Government of Canada estimates the lost revenue from the basic personal, spousal, and equivalent-to-spouse exemptions at \$26.1 billion in 2006 (Canada, department of Finance, 2006c: 18–22, table 1). The total value of the personal, spousal, and equivalent-to-spouse exemptions was estimated by dividing the \$26.1 billion by the lowest tax rate in 2006 (15.25%).

28 ◆ Note that indirect business taxes are levied by all three levels of government, federal, provincial, and local.

the equivalent amount of revenue from the tax base of $948.6 billion calculated above ($550.2 billion for individuals and $398.4 billion for businesses), a flat tax of 15.0% would be required.

Line 13 of table 5.4 shows that the existing federal corporate income-tax system generated $34.7 billion in revenue in 2006. The estimated revenue generated from the 15.0% business tax is $59.7 billion, nearly 72% more than is currently collected. On the other hand, the $82.4 billion in revenue generated from the 15.0% individual wage tax (table 5.4, line 10) is significantly less than the $107.4 billion currently collected from federal personal income taxes (table 5.4, line 12).

While the amount collected from individuals decreases and the amount collected from businesses increases, the Hall-Rabushka flat tax does not create a significant shift in taxes from wages to business (capital) income. Remember that the individual wage tax applies only to wages, salaries, and pensions. Canada's personal income-tax system currently taxes unincorporated business income, dividends, interest, and rental income that are all taxed under the business tax in the Hall-Rabushka flat tax. The main difference is that income generated from business activities and distributed to individuals is taxed and collected at the source of the income (business) rather than the destination (individual), as is the case in the current system.[29]

Lastly, the 15.0% flat tax will in all likelihood generate significantly more revenue for the federal government than the estimated $142.1 billion. That is, research has consistently shown that incentive-based tax reform results in greater revenue than forecasts predict. The reason for the increased revenue is that the improved incentives promote economic activities such as work effort, investment, and entrepreneurship that expand the tax base.[30] Incentive effects, which will increase actual

---

29 ◆ The initial change in a family's tax bill resulting from the implementation of a Hall-Rabushka flat tax will depend greatly on the composition of wages and salaries and business income. While we have not calculated estimates of which income groups would pay lower or higher taxes initially, once incomes increase as a result of improved incentives (see below) nearly all taxpayers are expected to benefit.

30 ◆ See chapter 2, Not All Taxes Are Created Equal; and Mankiw and Weinzierl, 2006.

revenues by expanding the size of the tax base, were not included in the calculations of the flat-tax rate. As a result, the federal government should be able to reduce the 15.0% tax rate and still collect the same amount of revenue it expected under the current income-tax system.

Capital gains

Capital gains[31] on rental property, structures (i.e. factories and buildings), machinery, and equipment are taxed under the Hall-Rabushka flat tax. Proceeds from the sale of these assets would be deemed business income and subject to the business tax.[32, 33]

At the individual level, however, income from capital gains is not taxed since it is already taxed at the business level (recall that the individual wage tax applies only to wages, salaries and private pensions). As a result, the Hall-Rabushka flat tax removes the double taxation of capital gains in the current tax system. Consider, for example, common stock or shares of a corporation. Since individual owners of common stock ultimately receive the after-tax income of the corporation, the stock price reflects the value of future expected after-tax income.[34] A capital gain occurs when the corporation's future expected after-tax income increases thereby increasing the value of the shares. Remember, when the increased income of the business actually materializes it will be subject to the business tax. Taxing a capital gain that might arise from the sale of the stock would result in the double taxation of one stream of income. Capital gains on owner-occupied residential property and personal-use property (i.e. cottages) are also not subject to taxes under the Hall-Rabushka flat tax.

---

31 ◆ A capital gain occurs if the value of the asset at the time of sale is greater than the original purchase price.

32 ◆ For example, every owner of rental property would be required to fill out a business tax return.

33 ◆ "Carried interest" would also be would be deemed business income and subject to the business tax. Carried interest is a share in a private equity, venture capital, or hedge fund and is calculated as a percentage of the profits generated by the fund. Under Canada's existing tax system, carried interest is taxed as a capital gain under certain partnership structures. See Morelli 2003, for further information.

34 ◆ That is, share prices reflect the capitalized value of after-tax business income.

Finally, it is important to recall that the fundamental principle of the Hall-Rabushka flat tax is to tax consumption. The tax base of the Hall-Rabushka flat tax, as presented above, is Gross Domestic Product (GDP), a measure of the total income produced in an economy, minus a few deductions. Estimates of Gross Domestic Product do not include capital gains.

Registered Retirement Savings Plans

To give Canadians incentives to save for retirement, Canada's current tax system allows individuals to establish and contribute to Registered Retirement Savings Plans (RRSPs).[35] Contributions of up to 18% of personal income to a maximum level ($19,000 in 2007) can be made to RRSP accounts each year and contributions are deductible from taxable income. In other words, RRSP contributions can reduce taxable income and income taxes paid. Income earned in RRSP accounts is also exempt from income taxes for the time the funds remain in the plan.[36] That is, RRSP accounts are tax-deferred savings accounts in that contributions made into the plan and returns on investments within the plan are not subject to income tax until money is withdrawn.

With a Hall-Rabushka flat tax, RRSP accounts would not be necessary because all savings by Canadians would receive the same advantages as those currently placed into RRSP accounts. That is, under the Hall-Rabushka flat tax there is no tax on income that is saved and the savings are tax-deferred in the sense that the tax is payable when the income is consumed. To see why RRSP accounts would be unnecessary, it is important understand how the flat tax excludes current savings. As discussed above, the Hall-Rabushka flat tax allows businesses to deduct investments in their entirety in the year purchased

---

35 ◆ Alternatively, Registered Pension Plans (RPPs) are employer-sponsored plans registered with Canada Revenue Agency. For individuals with RPPs, each years RRSP limit is reduced by the assessed value of benefits accrued in the previous year under an RPP.

36 ◆ Taxpayers are not permitted to keep contributing to their RRSPs past 71 years of age. At that time, taxpayers typically transfer the amount accumulated in to an RRIF (Registered Retirement Income Fund) or purchase an annuity. For more information see <http://www.cra-arc.gc.ca/tax/individuals/topics/rrsp/menu-e.html>.

(i.e. investments are expensed). Since all investments in an economy can ultimately be traced back to savings, the flat tax by exempting investment is a consumption tax.

For example, suppose a taxpayer earns $100, pays the $15 tax (assuming a flat tax of 15%), and puts the rest ($85) into the stock market. The business could buy $100 worth of equipment with the $85 from the individual because it receives a tax write-off worth $15. Even though the individual did not receive the deduction for purchasing the share, he receives the advantage of the investment expense. In effect, there is no tax for the saved income because the $15 in individual wage tax is offset by the $15 investment tax write-off. In other words, the incentive for the firm is passed onto the individual.[37] When the investment made by the business produces income, the earnings will be subject to the business tax if not reinvested and dispersed to the individual as dividends. If the earnings are re-invested, the amount of the investment is again exempt from the business tax. The flat tax, therefore, defers taxes because the tax is payable only when the earnings from the business are distributed to individuals and consumed.

In Canada's current tax system, individuals must deduct RRSP contributions from their income, save the income in a special account, and report any withdrawals from the account. The Hall-Rabushka flat tax provides the same advantages as RRSPs without the complex tax forms, record keeping, and other associated compliance costs. In addition, savings in RRSP accounts may not be beneficial for many Canadians with low and modest incomes in the current tax system since many will face higher tax rates in retirement.[38] This reduces the incentive for Canadians earning low and modest incomes to invest in RRSPs. Also, Canadians earning middle and upper incomes are limited in the amount they can save in RRSPs (18% of income to a maximum of $19,000 in 2007). The Hall-Rabushka flat tax excludes all current savings and treats all taxpayers equally since taxpayers face the same tax rate now as they will in retirement.[39]

---

37 ◆ The same analysis holds true for purchases of corporate bonds.

38 ◆ See Kesselman and Poschmann, 2001.

39 ◆ Assuming the flat-tax rate does not change.

Stock options

As part of their overall compensation, many Canadians are given stock options that enable them to purchase company shares at a set price in the future. If share prices increase, employees are able to buy the shares at the lower, predetermined price and sell at the current market price (called exercising an option). Under Canada's existing tax system, only half of the gain to the employee (difference between the market and purchase price) is subject to income taxes, which is equivalent to the treatment of capital gains.[40] Under the Hall-Rabushka flat tax, the full market value of the options is included in the taxpayer's compensation in the year they are received, whether or not they are exercised. Put differently, the estimated fair value of the options is included in the individual's salary and is therefore subject to the individual wage tax.[41]

Canadian banks

A short comment on banks is needed as they present a particular challenge to the Hall-Rabushka flat-tax model. The problem with banks is that they bundle services (i.e. processing deposits, clearing checks, preparing statements, providing ATM machines) with their financial products (i.e. interest earned on a deposit account). The price of these services is deducted from the market interest that depositors should earn, which is why deposit accounts pay interest rates significantly below market.

To understand the problem caused by bundling, suppose that the bank bundles enough services that none of its accounts pay any interest and that the bank invests all of the deposited money in government bonds. The bank would report no revenue on line 1 of its business tax return (figure 5.3) because financial income (interest) is not included in gross revenue. The bank could also report and deduct all

---

40 ◆ Certain conditions must be met in order to deduct half of the gain from taxable income. See Canada Revenue Agency, 1996 and Canada Revenue Agency, 2006a for further details.

41 ◆ A standard method of determining the fair value (price) of options would be required. A commonly used method is the Black-Scholes model.

of the costs associated with providing the bundled services including wages and investments in buildings and equipment. With no revenue and substantial costs, the bank could report negative taxable income every year.

The solution is to require banks to report the price of its services provided to depositors calculated as the difference between the market interest rate and the lower rate that the banks pay to depositors on accounts that have bundled services. The same requirement would apply to insurance companies and other businesses that bundle services with financial products.[42]

Multinational businesses

Canada currently maintains a complex system to deal with the business income generated from foreign operations or affiliates. Under the current system, Canada exempts active business earnings of foreign affiliates from Canadian tax.[43] Numerous changes to Canada's system of international taxation were announced in the 2007 federal budget, including better definitions of the active business income of a foreign affiliate and restrictions on the deductibility of interest paid on debt used to invest in foreign affiliates.[44] In addition, an advisory panel of tax experts is being created to undertake further study on measures to improve the fairness of Canada's system of international taxation.

With a Hall-Rabushka flat tax, Canada's complex system of international taxation is unnecessary as the tax applies only to the domestic operations of all businesses, whether Canadian or foreign owned. Only the revenue from the sales of goods and services sold within Canada or the values of products exported are included in the calculations of the business tax. Likewise, only the costs of labor, materials, and

---

42 ◆ Separate sets of rules for taxing financial intermediation services are common under a value-added tax (VAT). The basic principle of the flat tax is the same as value-added taxes as both are taxes on consumption. See Zee, 2004 for further information.

43 ◆ Active business income refers to income earned from the actual operations of a business as opposed to the income earned from financial investments (passive income).

44 ◆ For further information, see Canada, Department of Finance, 2007a.

other inputs purchased or imported into Canada are included. In other words, physical presence in Canada determines whether the firm is subject to the business tax. All overseas earnings of Canadian business would not be subject to the flat tax.

Employment Insurance and Canada Pension Plan premiums

The forms for reporting the federal individual wage tax presented above do not include Canada Pension Plan (CPP) and Employment Insurance (EI) premiums that Canadians are required to pay, though they could be added with little difficulty. In fact, both CPP and EI premiums are single-rate taxes. In 2007, employees and employers were required to pay Canada Pension Plan (CPP) premium rates of 4.95% on employment income ranging from $3,500 to $43,700. Employment Insurance (EI) premium rates were 1.80% of employment earnings from $0 to $40,000 for employees and 2.52% for employers. The employer's premiums are a tax-deductible expense for the employer and are not added to the employee's taxable income.

Under a Hall-Rabushka flat-tax, the employer's contribution to EI and CPP would not be deductible from the business tax, as is the case with all other non-wage benefits. In addition, the employee's contribution would be included in taxable income under the wage tax. CPP and EI benefits would not be taxed, however, when received.

Provincial flat taxes

While the Hall-Rabushka flat tax originally proposed for the United States focused exclusively on federal tax reform, the model is extended to the sub-national (provincial) level in this section. Provincial flat taxes are constructed and calculated in same manner as the federal flat tax. In addition, the provincial flat taxes raise the same amount of income-tax revenue (personal and corporate) as was raised by each province under the current system.

As is currently the case with provincial income taxes (with the exception of Quebec), the federal government's Canada Revenue Agency would administer and collect the individual wage tax. The federal individual wage-tax form (figure 5.2) could easily be augmented to include a few extra lines for provincial flat taxes. Alternatively, separate provincial forms identical to the federal form could be created. Canadians would pay the individual wage tax rate of the province where they resided on December 31.[45]

On the other hand, businesses would be required to submit business tax forms (returns) for each province in which they maintained a permanent establishment.[46] The provincial business tax return would similar to that presented in figure 5.3 above and again the federal government's Canada Revenue Agency could administer and collect the business tax.[47]

Since many businesses sell products and services in numerous provinces, gross revenue from the sales of goods and services would have to be allocated across those provinces. The method of allocating taxable income to provinces would be similar to the current system in which taxable income is allocated based on an average of the percentage of gross revenue reasonably attributable to a province and the percent of the business' total salaries and wages paid to employees in the province.[48]

Figure 5.4 and table 5.5 present the provincial and combined federal-provincial flat tax rates by province. Provincial flat taxes range from a low of 6.1% in Newfoundland and Labrador to 15.5% in Quebec.[49] Western Canadian provinces would require among the lowest provincial flat taxes with Alberta at 6.8%, Saskatchewan at 7.5%, and British

---

45 ◆ See Canada Revenue Agency, 2006a for further detail.

46 ◆ Canada Revenue Agency defines a permanent establishment as a fixed place of business such as an office, branch, oil well, farm, timberland, factory, workshop, warehouse, or mine.

47 ◆ Canada Revenue Agency currently administers corporate income taxes in all provinces, except for Quebec, Ontario, and Alberta. On October 6, 2006, the Government of Canada signed a Memorandum of Agreement with the Government of Ontario that will lead to the Canada Revenue Agency administering the provincial income tax in Ontario as well.

48 ◆ See Canada Revenue Agency, 2006b for more information.

49 ◆ Quebec's taxpayers face a higher provincial flat-tax rate in part due to the fact that Quebec opts out of certain federal-provincial programs for which the province must raise their own revenue. In return, Quebec's taxpayers face a lower federal flat-tax rate in lieu of cash that the other provinces receive from the federal government for these programs.

Figure 5.4: *Provincial and combined federal-provincial flat-tax rates, 2006*

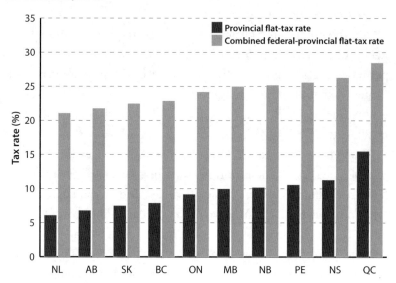

Source: Table 5.5.

Table 5.5: *Provincial and combined federal-provincial flat-tax rates, 2006*

	Provincial flat tax rate	Combined federal-provincial flat-tax rate
Newfoundland & Labrador	6.1%	21.1%
Prince Edward Island	10.6%	25.6%
Nova Scotia	11.3%	26.3%
New Brunswick	10.2%	25.2%
Quebec	15.5%	28.5%
Ontario	9.2%	24.2%
Manitoba	10.0%	25.0%
Saskatchewan	7.5%	22.5%
Alberta	6.8%	21.8%
British Columbia	7.9%	22.9%

Note: Quebec's taxpayers face lower federal taxes then taxpayers in other provinces because Quebec opts out of certain federal-provincial programs. Rather than receive federal cash for these programs, Quebec has chosen to raise their own revenue through increased provincial taxes. In lieu of cash, the federal government reduces federal taxes on residents of Québec.

Sources: Tables 5.4 and 5.6; calculations by the authors.

Columbia at 7.9%. Combined federal-provincial flat taxes range from 21.1% in Newfoundland and Labrador to 28.5% in Québec.[50]

Calculating revenue-neutral provincial flat tax rates

Table 5.6 presents calculations of revenue-neutral Hall-Rabushka flat taxes for each Canadian province. The tax base for the individual wage tax in each province is the sum of wages, salaries, and pension benefits less a personal exemption (allowance).[51] Personal exemptions vary from province to province, from a low of $7,410 in Newfoundland & Labrador to $14,899 in Alberta. Each province would also maintain their current exemptions for dependant spouses or equivalent-to-spouses.[52] For example, the maximum that a taxpayer in Alberta would have been permitted to earn tax free in 2006 was $29,798. Table 5.7 presents the personal exemption per taxpayer in each province including the basic personal exemption and the spousal and equivalent-to-spouse exemption amounts.

---

50 ◆ Quebec's taxpayers face lower federal taxes than taxpayers in other provinces because Quebec opts out of certain federal-provincial programs. Rather than receive federal cash for these programs, Quebec has chosen to raise their own revenue through increased provincial taxes. In lieu of cash, the federal government reduces federal taxes on residents of Québec.

51 ◆ To calculate total personal allowances in each province, tax expenditures of basic, spousal, and equivalent-to-spouse amount were calculated using Statistics Canada's Social Policy Simulation Database and Model (SPSD/M). The ratio of tax expenditures to personal income-tax revenues calculated using SPSD/M, was applied to the personal income-tax revenue data in the Provincial Economic Accounts (Statistics Canada, 2007c). The assumptions and calculations underlying the SPSD/M simulation results were prepared by The Fraser Institute and the responsibility for the use and interpretation of these data is entirely that of the authors.

52 ◆ Taxpayers are able to claim the spousal amount if they supported a spouse or common-law partner. Taxpayers are also able to claim the equivalent-to-spouse amount if, at any time during the year, they were single, divorced, separated, or widowed and, at that time supported a dependant (child under 18, your parent or grandparent, or 18 or older but mentally or physically infirm, and was related to you by blood, marriage, or adoption; and lived with you in a home that you maintained). See Canada Revenue Agency (2006b).

Table 5.6: Provincial flat-tax revenues compared with current provincial personal and corporate income tax revenues, 2006

	BC	AB	SK	MB	ON	QC	NB	NS	PEI	NL
Flat-tax rate										
	7.9%	6.8%	7.5%	10.0%	9.2%	15.5%	10.2%	11.3%	10.6%	6.1%
Income or revenue (millions of dollars)										
1 Gross domestic product										
	179,701	235,593	45,051	44,757	556,282	284,158	25,221	31,966	4,332	24,897
2 Indirect business tax (VAT plus excises)										
	15,452	9,649	3,496	3,811	43,961	25,250	2,417	3,103	468	1,776
3 Income in GDP, but not in tax base										
	6,891	5,265	956	1,197	12,671	5,227	743	1,141	161	499
4 Wages, salaries and pensions										
	91,125	96,596	18,237	22,271	297,646	150,868	13,328	17,241	2,293	8,327
5 Investment										
	19,022	52,700	6,124	5,333	52,698	27,199	2,819	3,642	395	2,879
6 Business-tax base (line 1 minus lines 2 through 5)										
	47,211	71,383	16,238	12,144	149,306	75,614	5,914	6,839	1,015	11,416
7 Business-tax revenue (flat tax rate multiplied by line 6)										
	3,714	4,859	1,216	1,209	13,784	11,747	601	773	108	695
8 Personal exemptions										
	34,292	35,482	6,477	7,045	83,933	55,660	4,754	5,229	915	2,692
9 Wage-tax base (line 4 less line 8)										
	56,833	61,114	11,759	15,227	213,712	95,208	8,574	12,012	1,378	5,635
10 Wage-tax revenue (flat tax rate multiplied by line 9)										
	4,471	4,160	880	1,516	19,730	14,791	871	1,357	146	343
11 Total flat-tax revenue (line 7 plus line 10)										
	8,186	9,019	2,096	2,724	33,514	26,538	1,472	2,130	254	1,038
12 Actual individual income tax										
	6,953	6,245	1,745	2,337	25,598	22,834	1,276	1,836	219	916
13 Actual corporate income tax										
	1,233	2,774	351	387	7,917	3,704	196	294	35	122
14 Total actual revenue (line 12 plus line 13)										
	8,186	9,019	2,096	2,724	33,514	26,538	1,472	2,130	254	1,038

Sources: Canada Revenue Agency, 2007b; Statistics Canada, 2007b, 2007c, 2007d, 2007e, 2007f; Statistics Canada, Public Institutions Division, 2007; Manitoba, Ministry of Finance, 2006: C18–C20; Ontario, Ministry of Finance, 2006a, 2006b: 87; Québec, Department of Finance, 2006a: 37–48, table 6; Saskatchewan, Ministry of Finance, 2006: 33–34; calculations by the authors.

Table 5.7: Basic personal allowance and spousal or equivalent-to-spouse allowances, in dollars, 2006

	Basic personal	Spousal or equivalent-to-spouse
Newfoundland & Labrador	7,410	6,055
Prince Edward Island	7,412	6,294
Nova Scotia	7,231	6,140
New Brunswick	8,061	6,845
Quebec	6,520	N/A
Ontario	8,377	7,113
Manitoba	7,734	6,482
Saskatchewan	8,589	8,589
Alberta	14,899	14,899
British Columbia	8,858	7,585
Federal Government	8,839	7,505

Note: Quebec does not provide spousal or equivalent-to-spouse amounts but rather allows transfers of non-refundable tax credits between spouses.

Source: PricewaterhouseCoopers, 2007; federal and provincial budgets, 2006, various jurisdictions.

The tax base for the provincial business tax is gross revenue from the sale of goods and services, less purchases of inputs from other firms, wages, salaries, and pensions paid to workers, and purchases of capital (plant, equipment, and land). Provincial Gross Domestic Product (GDP), the total value of goods and services produced within each province, is used to estimate total revenue from the sale of goods and services. As was the case for the federal calculations, GDP is adjusted for indirect business taxes that are included in GDP but not should be included in the business-tax base.[53] In addition, provincial GDP includes an estimate of the rental value of houses owned and lived in by families (imputed rental income of owner-occupied housing), which must be removed to calculate the business-tax base.

---

53 ◆ Indirect business taxes include all taxes that represent a business cost (i.e. sales taxes, excise taxes, and import duties) minus subsidies from government to businesses.

Lastly, it is important to emphasize again that the flat taxes calculated for each province would likely generate significantly more revenue for provincial government than that presented on line 14 in table 5.6. Economic research presented in chapter 1 suggests that the tax base in each province will increase as a result of improved incentives for productive economic behavior. Therefore, the revenues generated by the provincial rates in table 5.5 would in all likelihood be larger than forecast.

4 ◆ Economic impacts of a Hall-Rabushka flat tax for Canada

Reforming Canada's personal and business income-tax systems by implementing a Hall-Rabushka flat tax would have a significant impact on the Canadian economy. Most critically, the flat tax proposed in section 3 would improve the incentives Canadians have to engage in productive economic behavior. Improved incentives would result in increased work effort, savings and investment, and entrepreneurial activity, and a much improved outlook for Canada's future economic performance.

First, the Hall-Rabushka flat tax proposed for Canada in section 3 would eliminate Canada's increasing marginal personal income-tax rates.[54] When deciding to increase the amount of time spent working or the level of effort exerted, individuals are influenced by the amount of after-tax income produced. Evidence from economic research presented in chapter 1 indicates that increasing or progressive marginal tax rates act as penalty to increased work effort. That is, increasing the tax rate that individuals face as they earn more income reduces their incentive to increase the total number of hours worked and their overall work effort. By eliminating increasing marginal tax rates, the Hall-Rabushka flat tax would encourage Canadians to reach their

---

54 ◆ The flat tax has some marginality as a result of the personal exemption. That is, there are two rates: 0% up to the exemption threshold and the flat tax rate on income earned above the threshold.

full economic potential. Estimates for the United States by Hall and Rabushka indicate that the total annual output of goods and services produced would increase by about 3% due to the elimination of dis-incentives for work.

The Hall-Rabushka flat tax would also eliminate high marginal tax rates faced by many Canadians with low and moderate incomes. These high marginal tax rates result from many federal and provincial tax credits and benefits (property-tax credits, child tax benefits, and the Goods and Services Tax [GST] and provincial sales-tax credits) being income tested; that is, the benefits of these credits are reduced sig-nificantly as an individual's income increases. The reduction in ben-efits, often referred to as "claw-backs," reduces the financial reward for increased work effort. Professor Jack Mintz, one of Canada's lead-ing tax experts has shown that marginal tax rates in some provinces (including provincial and federal rates) approach 80% for families with incomes of around $40,000 (Mintz, 2006). In other words, a family can lose up to 80¢ of each additional dollar of income it earns as a result of taxes and the reduction in the value of tax credits and benefits. These high marginal rates are eliminated in the Hall-Rabushka flat tax pre-sented above because nearly all exemptions, deductions, and credits in the current system are eliminated. As a result, the incentives for Canadians with low and modest incomes to increase their work effort and the number of hours worked would be significantly improved.

The elimination of progressive marginal tax rates would also increase the level of entrepreneurial activity in the Canadian economy. A relatively recent paper published in the *American Economic Review* by economists William Gentry and Glenn Hubbard (2000) analyzed US data over the period 1979 to 1992 and found that a more progres-sive tax structure reduced the probability of an individual becom-ing an entrepreneur (self-employed). Chapter 1 of this book reviews the growing body of research on the impact of taxes on the level of entrepreneurship.

In addition to increasing the level of entrepreneurial activity through the elimination of progressive tax rates, the Hall-Rabushka flat tax would encourage entrepreneurship by eliminating the double taxation on business income in the current tax system. Many entrepreneurs develop their innovations with the help of investors who provide financing in return for an equity position (ownership shares) in the business. Under the current tax system, when new businesses mature and begin to generate earnings, the earnings are subject to business income taxes and personal income taxes. In addition, entrepreneurs and financiers face capital gains taxes if they sell their portion of the business at a profit. The elimination of the double taxation of business income under the Hall-Rabushka flat tax would increase the return on the efforts of entrepreneurs and their financiers and have a positive impact on the level and financing of entrepreneurship.

Perhaps most importantly, the Hall-Rabushka flat tax would have a significant impact on investment (capital formation) in Canada. First, the current tax system subsidizes certain investments through tax incentives that channel investment into less productive uses. By eliminating such incentives, the Hall-Rabushka flat tax would allow market decisions to direct investment to opportunities that provided the highest expected return. In addition, the Hall-Rabushka flat tax allows for the full deductibility of the value of all capital investments (plant, equipment, and land) in the year of purchase. This would reduce the tax burden on investments and significantly increase the amount of investment undertaken by businesses. In the current tax system, businesses are only able to write off or deduct the percentage of the total cost of purchasing plants and equipment that is determined by the government's capital-cost-allowance (CCA) rates.[55] Allowing business to expense their capital investments at full value would defer taxation until the asset produces earnings and would encourage investment.

Finally, Hall and Rabushka conclude that there would be an immediate decrease in interest rates under their flat-tax regime. In the current tax system, businesses are able to deduct interest payments from earnings and individuals are forced to pay personal income taxes on interest income. As a result, businesses that borrow accept high interest rates because of the deductibility and individual Canadian lenders demand high interest rates because interest income is taxed. Under

---

55 ◆ Capital-cost-allowance (CCA) rates are generally set so as to spread the deduction over the useful life of the asset.

the Hall-Rabushka flat tax, interest payments are not deductible from income and interest income is not taxed at the individual level, which puts downward pressure on interest rates. The reduction in interest rates would have a positive impact on the amount that businesses borrow to invest in capital.

All told, Hall and Rabushka estimate that a federal flat tax in the United States would increase the total annual output of goods and services produced by 6%: 3% from improved incentives to work and 3% from improved incentives for investment and entrepreneurial activity. If the same held true for Canada, the increase in total output (GDP) as a result of the federal 15.0% flat tax would amount to $2,646 per Canadian. Provincial flat taxes would also contribute significantly to this estimate.

5 ◆ Conclusion

Canada's current income-tax system is neither simple, efficient, nor equitable. Taxpayers spend significant resources complying with, and indirectly financing, the administration of our complex tax system. The tax system also reduces economic growth by creating strong disincentives to work hard, save, invest, and engage in entrepreneurial activities. In addition, the tax system fails to ensure that individuals and households with similar incomes face similar tax burdens.

The Hall-Rabushka flat tax proposed in this chapter calls for an entirely new income-tax system with a low rate on a broad definition of income in which all income would be taxed only once. The proposed Canadian flat tax would significantly improve the incentives to engage in productive economic behavior and reduce the costs to comply with, and administer, the tax system. All distortions currently caused by increasing marginal rates and special tax incentives would be eliminated. And as a result of a personal exemption, the tax would be progressive because the percentage of income paid in taxes would increase with income. Above all, the Hall-Rabushka flat tax would result in a substantially higher level of national output and an improved standard of living.

References

Alberta, Ministry of Finance (2006). *2006–09 Fiscal Plan*.

Alberta, Ministry of Finance (2007). *Managing Our Growth, Budget 2007*.

British Columbia, Ministry of Finance (2006). *Budget and Fiscal Plan 2006/07–2008/09*.

Canada, Department of Finance (2006). *The Budget Plan 2006: Focusing on Priorities*.

Canada, Department of Finance (2007a). *The Budget Plan 2007: Aspire to a Stronger, Safer, Better Canada*. <http://www.budget. gc.ca/2007/pdf/bp2007e.pdf>.

Canada, Department of Finance (2007b). *Strong Leadership. A Better Canada. Economic Statement 2007*. <http://www.fin.gc.ca/ budtoce/2007/eco7_e.html>.

Canada, Department of Finance (2007c). *Tax Expenditures and Evaluations 2006*.

Canada Revenue Agency (1996). *CRA Income Tax Interpretation Bulletin: Benefits to Employees – Stock Options*. <http://www.cra-arc.gc.ca>.

Canada Revenue Agency (2006a). *General Income Tax and Benefit Guide – 2006*. <http://www.cra-arc.gc.ca/E/pub/tg/5000-g/5000-g-06e.pdf>.

Canada Revenue Agency (2006b). *T2 Corporation – Income Tax Guide 2006*. <http://www.cra-arc.gc.ca/E/pub/tg/t4012/t4012-07e.pdf>.

Canada Revenue Agency (2007a). *Federal and provincial/territorial tax rates.* <http://www.cra-arc.gc.ca/tax/individuals/faq/taxrates-e.html#federal>.

Canada Revenue Agency (2007b). *Income Statistics 2007 Edition – 2005 Tax Year, Interim Statistics – Universe Data.* <http://www.cra-arc.gc.ca/agency/stats/interim-e.html>.

Clemens, Jason, and Niels Veldhuis (2003). Who Pays Business Taxes? A Different View. *Fraser Forum* (October): 30–31.

Clemens, Jason, and Niels Veldhuis (2005). *Growing Small Businesses in Canada: Removing the Tax Barrier.* The Fraser Institute.

Clemens, Jason, Niels Veldhuis, and Milagros Palacios (2007). *Tax Efficiency—Not All Taxes Are Created Equal.* Studies in Economic Prosperity 4. The Fraser Institute.

Cumming, Dougals, and Keith Godin (2007). *Crowding Out Private Equity: Canadian Evidence.* The Fraser Institute.

Emes Joel, and Jason Clemens with Patrick Basham and Dexter Samida (2001). *Flat Tax: Principles and Issues.* Critical Issues Bulletin. The Fraser Institute.

Godin, Keith, Niels Veldhuis, and Jason Clemens (2007). *The Economic Costs of Capital Gains Taxes.* The Fraser Institute.

Gentry, William, and Glenn Hubbard (2000). Tax Policy and Entrepreneurial Entry. *American Economic Review* 90, 2: 283–87.

Grubel, Herbert G., ed. (2003). *Tax Reform in Canada: Our Path to Greater Prosperity.* The Fraser Institute.

Hall, Robert E., and Alvin Rabushka (2007). *The Flat Tax*. Second Edition. Hoover Institution Press. <http://www.hooverpress.org/productdetails.cfm?PC=1274>.

Kesselman, Jonathan, and Finn Poschmann (2001). *A New Option for Retirement Savings: Tax-Prepaid Savings Plans*. Commentary 149. C.D. Howe Institute.

Manitoba, Ministry of Finance, 2006. *Budget 2006*.

Mankiw, Gregory, and Matthew Weinzierl (2006). Dynamic Scoring: A Back of the Envelope Guide. *Journal of Public Economics* 90, 8-9: 1415–33.

Mintz, Jack M (2006). *The 2006 Tax Competitiveness Report: Proposals for Pro-GrowthTax Reform*. Commentary 239 (September). C.D. Howe Institute. <http://www.cdhowe.org>.

Morelli, Yvette (2003). Structuring Venture Capital Funds. *Canadian Tax Journal* 51, 2: 806–62. Canadian Tax Foundation. <http://www.ctf.ca/pdf/ctjpdf/2003ctj2_morelli.pdf>.

New Brunswick, Department of Finance (2006). *Budget 2006–2007*.

Newfoundland & Labrador, Department of Finance (2006). *Budget 2006*.

Nova Scotia, Department of Finance (2006). *Budget 2006–2007*.

Ontario, Ministry of Finance (2006a). *Economic Outlook and Fiscal Review*.

Ontario, Ministry of Finance (2006b). *2006 Budget*.

PricewaterhouseCoopers (2007). *Putting the Puzzle Together - Tax Facts and Figures: Canada 2007*. <http://www.pwc.com>.

Prince Edward Island, Department of the Provincial Treasury (2006). *Budget 2006–2007.*

Québec, Department of Finance (2006a). *Tax Expenditures 2006.*

Québec, Department of Finance (2006b). *2006–2007 Budget.*

Rabushka, Alvin (1987). *Reforming the White Paper on Tax Reform.* Critical Issues Bulletin. The Fraser Institute.

Saskatchewan, Ministry of Finance (2006). *Budget and Performance Plan 2006–2007.*

Statistics Canada (2007a). *Labour Force Historical Review 2006.* CD-ROM-71F0004XCB. Statistics Canada.

Statistics Canada (2007b). *National Income and Expenditure Accounts, Quarterly Estimates, First Quarter 2007.* Catalogue No. 13-001-XIB. Statistics Canada.

Statistics Canada (2007c). *Provincial Economic Accounts.* Statistics Canada.

Statistics Canada (2007d). *Sector Accounts, All Levels of Government, Quarterly (Dollars).* CANSIM table 380-0007. Statistics Canada.

Statistics Canada (2007e). *Income and Expenditure Sub-sector Accounts, Federal Government, Quarterly (Dollars).* CANSIM table 380-0034. Statistics Canada.

Statistics Canada (2007f). Social Policy Simulation Database and Model (SPSD/M). Version 14.2. Statistics Canada.

Statistics Canada, Public Institutions Division (2007). Financial Management System. Statistics Canada.

Solberg, Monte (2000). *Solution 17: The Single Rate Tax*. The Canadian Alliance.

Treff, Karin, and David B. Perry (2005). *Finances of the Nation 2005*. <http://www.ctf.ca>.

Veldhuis, Niels, and Jason Clemens (2004). Does Canada Have a Marriage Tax Penalty? *Fraser Forum* (March): 9–12.

Veldhuis, Niels, and Jason Clemens (2006). *Productivity, Prosperity and Business Taxes*. Studies in Economic Prosperity 3. The Fraser Institute.

Veldhuis, Niels, and Michael Walker (2006). *Tax Facts 14*. The Fraser Institute.

Zee, Howell H. (2004). *A New Approach to Taxing Financial Intermediation Service under a Value-Added Tax*. IMF Working Paper 119. International Monetary Fund

Publishing information

Distribution

This publication is also available from <http://www.fraserinstitute.org> in Portable Document Format (PDF) and can be read with Adobe Acrobat® or with Adobe Reader®, which is available free of charge from Adobe Systems Inc. To down-load Adobe Reader, go to this link: <http://www.adobe.com/products/acrobat/readstep2.html> with your browser. We encourage you to install the most recent version.

Ordering publications

For information about ordering the printed publications of The Fraser Institute, please contact the publications coordinator

- ◆ e-mail: sales@fraserinstitute.ca
- ◆ telephone: 604.688.0221 ext. 580 or, toll free, 1.800.665.3558 ext. 580
- ◆ fax: 604.688.8539.

Media

For media enquiries, please contact our Communications Department

- ◆ telephone: 604.714.4582
- ◆ e-mail: communications@fraserinstitute.ca.

Website

To learn more about The Fraser Institute and to read our publications on line, please visit our website at <http://fraserinstitute.org>.

Copyright

Date of issue: February 2008

Editing, design, and production: Lindsey Thomas Martin

Cover design: Bill Ray

Image for front cover: ©Adam Korzekwa, iStockphoto

About The Fraser Institute

Our vision is a free and prosperous world where individuals benefit from greater choice, competitive markets, and personal responsibility. Our mission is to measure, study, and communicate the impact of competitive markets and government interventions on the welfare of individuals.

Founded in 1974, we are an independent research and educational organization with offices in Calgary, Montréal, Tampa, Toronto, and Vancouver, and international partners in over 70 countries. Our work is financed by tax-deductible contributions from thousands of individuals, organizations, and foundations. In order to protect its independence, the Institute does not accept grants from government or contracts for research.

菲沙研究所的願景乃一自由而昌盛的世界，當中每個人得以從更豐富的選擇、具競爭性的市場及自我承擔責任而獲益。我們的使命在於量度、研究並使人知悉競爭市場及政府干預對個人福祉的影響。

創辦於1974年，我們乃一獨立的研究及教育機構，在卡加利、滿地可、坦帕、多倫多及溫哥華均設有辦事處，並在超過七十個國家擁有國際伙伴。我們的工作得到不同人仕、機構及基金透過可免稅捐獻資助。為了保持其獨立性，本研究所不接受政府的撥款或研究合約。

Nous envisageons un monde libre et prospère, où chaque personne bénéficie d'un plus grand choix, de marchés concurrentiels et de responsabilités individuelles. Notre mission consiste à mesurer, à étudier et à communiquer l'effet des marchés concurrentiels et des interventions gouvernementales sur le bien-être des individus.

Fondé en 1974, notre Institut existe en tant qu'organisme indépendant de recherches et établissement éducatif. Nous avons des bureaux à Calgary, à Montréal, à Tampa, à Toronto, et à Vancouver, ainsi que des associés internationaux dans plus de 70 pays. Notre œuvre est financée par la contribution déductible d'impôt de milliers de personnes, d'organismes et de fondations. Pour protéger son indépendance, l'Institut Fraser n'accepte ni subvention gouvernementale ni recherche sous contrat.

Nuestra visión es un mundo libre y próspero donde los individuos se beneficien de una mayor oferta, la competencia en los mercados y la responsabilidad individual. Nuestra misión es medir, estudiar y comunicar el impacto de la competencia en los mercados y la intervención gubernamental en el bienestar de los individuos.

Fundado en 1974, nuestro instituto es una organización independiente dedicada a la investigación y educación, con oficinas en Calgary, Montréal, Tampa, Toronto y Vancouver; además de contar con asociados internacionales en más de 70 países. Nuestro trabajo es financiado por donaciones voluntarias de miles de individuos, organizaciones y fundaciones. A fin de mantener nuestra independencia, el Instituto no acepta subvenciones del gobierno ni contratos para realizar trabajos de investigación.

Supporting The Fraser Institute

For information about how to support The Fraser Institute, please contact

- ◆ Development Department, The Fraser Institute
  Fourth Floor, 1770 Burrard Street
  Vancouver, British Columbia, V6J 3G7 Canada
- ◆ telephone, toll-free: 1.800.665.3558 ext. 586
- ◆ e-mail: development@fraserinstitute.ca

Calgary
- ◆ telephone: 403.216.7175 ext. 227
- ◆ fax: 403.234.9010

Montréal
- ◆ telephone: 514.281.9550 ext. 303
- ◆ fax: 514.281.9464
- ◆ e-mail: montreal@fraserinstitute.ca.

Tampa, USA
- ◆ telephone: 813.961.6543
- ◆ fax: 636.773.2152
- ◆ e-mail: Joyce.Weaver@fraserinstitute.org.

Toronto
- ◆ telephone: 416.363.6575 ext. 232
- ◆ fax: 416.934.1639.

Vancouver
- ◆ telephone: 604.688.0221 ext. 586
- ◆ fax: 604.688.8539